第2版
2nd Edition

"一带一路"篇
THE BELT AND
ROAD INITIATIVE

中国关键词

KEYWORDS TO UNDERSTAND CHINA

权 威 解 读 当 代 中 国

中国外文出版发行事业局(CICG)
当代中国与世界研究院(ACCWS)
中国翻译研究院(CATL)

新世界出版社
NEW WORLD PRESS

First Edition 2017
Second Edition 2019

Compiled by
China International Communications Group, Academy of Contemporary China and World Studies and China Academy of Translation

Translated by
Han Qingyue and Cai Lijian

English text edited by
David W. Ferguson and Xu Mingqiang

ISBN 978-7-5104-6737-0

Published by
NEW WORLD PRESS
24 Baiwanzhuang Street, Beijing 100037, China

Distributed by
NEW WORLD PRESS
24 Baiwanzhuang Street, Beijing 100037, China
Tel: 86-10-68995968
Fax: 86-10-68998705
Website: http://www.nwp.com.cn
E-mail: nwpcd@sina.com

Printed in the People's Republic of China

Keywords to Understand China
The Belt and Road Initiative
Editorial Committee

前 言

《中国关键词："一带一路"篇》多文种系列图书是"中国关键词多语对外传播平台"项目成果。

"中国关键词多语对外传播平台"是中国外文出版发行事业局、当代中国与世界研究院、中国翻译研究院联合组织实施的国家重点项目，主要围绕习近平新时代中国特色社会主义思想，进行中文词条专题编写、解读以及多语种编译，通过平面、网络和移动社交平台等多媒体、多渠道、多形态及时持续对外发布，旨在以国外受众易于阅读和理解的方式，阐释中国理念和中国思想，解读中国政策和中国发展道路。

为了使读者更全面、客观地了解"一带一路"倡议，《中国关键词》项目组联合中央相关部委、涉外新闻媒体、科研机构以及高等院校的研究及翻译专家，系统梳理、专题编写、编译出版了《中国关键词："一带一路"篇》中外对照多文种系列图书，涵盖英语、法语、俄语、西班牙语、阿拉伯语、德语、葡语、意大利语、日语、韩语、越南语、印尼语、土耳其语、哈萨克语 14 个语种。

由于能力及时间所限，在中文词条选择和编写这些“关键词”时，难免挂一漏万，表述也可能存在偏颇，尤其是在介绍相关国家或组织倡议和前期合作项目时，只提供了部分线索；外文译文表达也可能多有不足，仅供阅读参考，欢迎读者指正。

讲故事需要关键词，讲好中国故事需要中国关键词。让我们用“中国关键词”点击中国、沟通世界。

INTRODUCTION

Keywords to Understand China: the Belt and Road Initiative is a selection of "China Keywords" entries included in an eponymous multilingual platform.

The "China Keywords" platform is a national-level project undertaken by the China International Communications Group, Academy of Contemporary China and World Studies and China Academy of Translation. It offers expert interpretation of Xi Jinping Thought on Socialism with Chinese Characteristics for a New Era through multiple means of the media, and serves an international audience as a window into China's political thinking, policies, and approach to development.

This booklet is compiled to help readers better understand China's Belt and Road Initiative. During the compilation process, the "China Keywords" project team worked closely with experts from relevant government departments, news outlets, research institutes and institutions of higher learning. Entries are grouped under thematic headings and presented in Arabic, English, French, German, Indonesian Bahasa, Italian, Japanese, Kazak, Korean, Portuguese, Russian, Spanish, Turkish, and Vietnamese, as well as the original Chinese.

Due to the scope of the work and its tight schedule, oversights and inaccuracies are possible in our selection of entries, particularly our inclusion of the initiatives of other countries and organizations, and preliminary projects. Our translations may also leave room for improvement. Comments and suggestions are welcome for future revisions.

Keywords are key to telling a story. "China Keywords" are key to telling the story of China. We hope that these "China Keywords" will help build a bridge of understanding between China and the rest of the world.

CONTENTS
目 录

基本概念 · The Architecture

建设目标 · Building Blocks

合作重点 · Priority Areas of Cooperation

“走廊”建设 · Economic Corridors

合作机制 · Cooperation Mechanisms

其他国家或组织倡议 · Similar Initiatives

合作案例 · Projects Under Way

基本概念

The Architecture

“一带一路”

“一带一路”是“丝绸之路经济带”和“21世纪海上丝绸之路”的简称。2013年9月和10月，中国国家主席习近平出访中亚和东南亚时，分别提出了与相关国家共同建设“丝绸之路经济带”和“21世纪海上丝绸之路”的倡议。该倡议以实现“政策沟通、设施联通、贸易畅通、资金融通、民心相通”为主要内容，以“共商、共建、共享”为原则，实实在在地造福沿线国家和人民。“一带一路”主要涵盖东亚、东南亚、南亚、西亚、中亚和中东欧等国家和地区。“一带一路”建设符合有关各方共同利益，顺应地区和全球合作潮流，得到了沿线国家的积极响应。截至2019年3月，中国已经与123个国家和29个国际组织签署了152份共建“一带一路”的协议，签署范围自亚欧大陆拓展至非洲、拉美和加勒比地区、南太平洋地区；同30多个国家开展机制化产能合作，在共建国家建设了82个经贸合作区，为当地创造24.4万个就业岗位，

Belt and Road Initiative

The Belt and Road Initiative – China's proposal to build a Silk Road Economic Belt and a 21st Century Maritime Silk Road in cooperation with related countries – was unveiled by Chinese President Xi Jinping during his visits to Central and Southeast Asia in September and October 2013. The initiative focuses on promoting policy coordination, connectivity of infrastructure and facilities, unimpeded trade, financial integration, and closer people-to-people ties through a consultative process and joint efforts, with the goal of bringing benefits to all.

The initiative covers primarily East Asia, Southeast Asia, South Asia, West Asia, Central Asia, and Central and Eastern Europe. It reflects a convergence of interests and an increasing need for regional and global cooperation. The response from countries along the proposed Belt and Road has been enthusiastic.

The Belt and Road Initiative has driven new advances in opening up. By March 2019, China had signed 152 cooperation agreements with 123 countries and 29 international organizations from Asia, Europe, Africa, Latin America and the Caribbean, and South Pacific, and carried out industrial cooperation projects with more than 30 countries. It has co-built 82 economic and trade cooperation zones with other countries,

上交东道国税费22.1亿美元，推动形成了以“一带一路”为引领的对外开放新格局。共建“一带一路”已经写入联合国大会、安理会等重要决议，联合国安理会通过的第2344号决议，呼吁国际社会通过“一带一路”建设加强区域经济合作。

which have created 244,000 jobs for the local people, and generated US$2.21 billion taxes to the host countries.

The UN General Assembly and Security Council have made reference to the initiative in some of their resolutions. General Assembly resolution 2344, for instance, called on the international community to increase regional economic cooperation through the Belt and Road Initiative.

丝绸之路经济带

2100多年前，中国汉代的张骞两次出使西域，开启了中国同中亚各国友好交往的大门，开辟出一条横贯东西、连接欧亚的丝绸之路。千百年来，在这条古老的丝绸之路上，各国人民共同谱写出辉煌灿烂的友好篇章。为了使欧亚各国经济联系更加紧密、相互合作更加深入、发展空间更加广阔，2013年9月7日，习近平主席在哈萨克斯坦纳扎尔巴耶夫大学发表演讲时提出，用创新的合作模式，共同建设丝绸之路经济带，以点带面，从线到片，逐步形成区域大合作。丝绸之路经济带东边牵着亚太经济圈，西边系着发达的欧洲经济圈，被认为是“世界上最长、最具有发展潜力的经济大走廊”。

Silk Road Economic Belt

The Silk Road first emerged more than 2,100 years ago during the Han Dynasty after China's envoy Zhang Qian (164-114 BC) twice visited Central Asia. It became a bridge between East and West, opening the door to friendly engagement between China and Central Asia. For two millennia, countless tales of everlasting friendship between peoples have been woven into this ancient network.

In a speech at Kazakhstan's Nazarbayev University on September 7, 2013, President Xi Jinping proposed building a Silk Road Economic Belt to expand Eurasian economic cooperation. An innovative cooperative approach was outlined, starting with individual projects that are expected to help spur larger-scale regional cooperative development. The proposed economic belt is considered the longest economic corridor in the world – and potentially the most dynamic – connecting the Asia-Pacific region in the east with developed European economies in the west.

21世纪海上丝绸之路

自秦汉时期开通以来，海上丝绸之路一直是东西方经济文化交流融通的重要桥梁。东南亚地区是海上丝绸之路的重要枢纽和组成部分。在中国与东盟建立战略伙伴关系10周年之际，为了进一步加强双方的海上合作，发展双方的海洋合作伙伴关系，构建更加紧密的命运共同体，2013年10月3日，习近平主席在印度尼西亚国会发表演讲时提出，共同建设21世纪海上丝绸之路。21世纪海上丝绸之路的战略合作伙伴并不仅限于东盟，而是以点带线，以线带面，串起联通东盟、南亚、西亚、北非、欧洲等各大经济板块的市场链，发展面向南海、太平洋和印度洋的战略合作经济带。

21st Century Maritime Silk Road

Formed during the Qin and Han Dynasties (221 BC-AD 220), the Maritime Silk Road has always played an important role in economic and cultural exchanges and integration between East and West. And Southeast Asia has always been a nexus of this interaction. On the occasion of the 10th Anniversary of the China-ASEAN Strategic Partnership, President Xi Jinping proposed jointly building a 21st Century Maritime Silk Road in his speech to the Indonesian parliament on October 3, 2013. The initiative aims to boost China-ASEAN maritime cooperation and forge closer ties in a community of a shared future. It calls for joint efforts across the region and beyond.

Starting with the launch of individual projects that are expected to help spur a wider range of cooperative activities, it envisions a network of interconnected markets linking the ASEAN, South Asia, West Asia, North Africa, and Europe, and a strategic partnership for the South China Sea and the Pacific and Indian oceans.

丝路精神

古丝绸之路绵亘万里，延续千年，不仅是商业通道，更重要的是它所承载的丝路精神。古丝绸之路作为人文社会的交往平台，多民族、多种族、多宗教、多文化在此交汇融合，在长期交往过程中，各国之间积淀形成了以和平合作、开放包容、互学互鉴、互利共赢为核心的丝路精神。这一精神，也是现代国际社会交往的最基本原则之一。

Spirit of the Silk Road

The ancient Silk Road was a trade route that spanned thousands of miles. More than this, it had been a platform for people-to-people and cultural exchanges, where ethnic, racial, religious and cultural convergence took place down the centuries. For millennia, interaction along this route has shaped the Silk Road spirit, which is embodied in peace and cooperation, openness and inclusiveness, mutual learning and mutual benefit. Such an understanding also informs one of the fundamental principles for international interaction today.

丝路基金

2014年11月8日，习近平主席宣布，中国将出资400亿美元成立丝路基金。2014年12月29日，丝路基金有限责任公司在北京注册成立。丝路基金为“一带一路”沿线国基础设施建设、资源开发、产业合作等有关项目提供投融资支持。它同其他全球和区域多边开发银行的关系是相互补充而不是相互替代的。它将在现行国际经济金融秩序下运行。丝路基金绝非简单的经济援助，而是通过互联互通为相关国家的发展创造新的重大发展机遇。丝路基金是开放的，欢迎亚洲域内外的投资者积极参与。

Silk Road Fund

The Silk Road Fund was established in Beijing on December 29, 2014, following President Xi Jinping's announcement on November 8 that China would contribute US$40 billion for this purpose. The Fund will support infrastructure and resource development and industrial cooperation in the countries along the land and sea Silk Roads. It will complement rather than serve as a substitute for other global and regional multilateral development banks, and will operate under the existing international economic and financial order.

Instead of simply dispensing economic aid, the Fund will exploit increased connectivity to create major development opportunities for all. It is an open scheme and welcomes the participation of investors from Asia and beyond.

亚洲基础设施投资银行

2013年10月，中国国家主席习近平提出了筹建亚洲基础设施投资银行（简称亚投行）的倡议。在历经800余天筹备后，由中国倡议成立、57国共同筹建的亚投行于2015年12月25日在北京宣告成立。2016年1月16日，亚投行举行了开业仪式，习近平主席出席并致辞。亚投行是一个政府间性质的区域多边开发机构，重点支持基础设施建设，这是首个由中国倡议设立的多边金融机构。截至2018年12月19日，共有93个成员，总成员数仅次于世界银行，涵盖了西方七国集团中的5个、二十国集团中的16个和联合国安理会常任理事国中的4个。亚投行初期投资重点领域包括能源与电力、交通和电信、农村和农业基础设施、供水与污水处理、环境保护、城市发展以及物流等，首批贷款计划已于2016年6月获准。

Asian Infrastructure Investment Bank

The idea of creating a new multilateral bank, the Asian Infrastructure Investment Bank (AIIB), was first evinced by President Xi Jinping of China in October 2013. After more than 800 days of combined preparatory efforts by 57 countries, the AIIB was formally established, in accordance with China's proposal, on December 25, 2015 in Beijing. The bank held its opening ceremony on January 16, 2016, and President Xi Jinping made a speech at the ceremony.

The AIIB is a regional inter-governmental development institution focused on supporting infrastructure development. It is the first multinational financial institution sponsored by China. As of December 19, 2018, the bank's membership had reached 93, second only to that of the World Bank. Among its members, there are five G7 members, 16 G20 members, and four UN Security Council permanent members.

Among other sectors, the bank will initially invest in energy and electricity, transport, telecommunications, rural and agricultural infrastructure, water supply and sewerage, environmental protection, urban development, and logistics. The first batch of loans was approved in June 2016.

推进“一带一路”建设工作领导小组

“一带一路”建设是一项宏大的系统工程，仅在中国国内，它所涉及的政府机构、企业和社会组织就非常广泛，“一带一路”建设的很多项目跨越时间也很长，因此需要加强组织和领导，统筹做好各方面的工作。为此，中国政府专门成立了推进“一带一路”建设工作领导小组，负责审议“一带一路”建设工作的重大规划、政策、项目和相关问题，指导和协调落实“一带一路”合作倡议。该领导小组现任组长由中共中央政治局常委、国务院副总理韩正担任。外交部、商务部等是该小组的成员单位。该小组办公室设在国家发展和改革委员会，具体承担领导小组日常工作。此外，在中国的相关部委和省（自治区、直辖市）政府层面，也成立了推进“一带一路”建设工作领导小组，一般是由相关部委和省（自治区、直辖市）主要领导担任负责人。

Steering Group for the Belt and Road Initiative

Implementing the Belt and Road Initiative is a massive undertaking. Domestically, it involves a wide range of government agencies, businesses and civil society organizations. Many projects are likely to extend over years. Integrated planning and guidance are essential. A steering group for the Belt and Road Initiative has thus been established at the national level to study important issues related to planning, policy, and projects, and to provide guidance and coordination in the implementation of the initiative. Currently headed by Vice Premier Han Zheng, the group consists of representatives from China's government agencies including the Ministry of Foreign Affairs and the Ministry of Commerce. The secretariat of the steering group, which is placed under the National Development and Reform Commission, is responsible for the day-to-day work of the group. Ministerial and provincial level steering groups have also been established, each headed by a key member of the leadership team of the ministry or province (autonomous region or municipality) concerned.

《推动共建丝绸之路经济带和21世纪海上丝绸之路的愿景与行动》

2015年3月28日，《推动共建丝绸之路经济带和21世纪海上丝绸之路的愿景与行动》白皮书在博鳌亚洲论坛上正式发布。这份官方文件得到国务院授权，由国家发展和改革委员会、外交部和商务部共同编写。该文件简明扼要地阐述了"一带一路"倡议的背景、原则、框架思想、合作重点与机制等。文件强调，"一带一路"建设坚持共商、共建、共享原则，以实现"政策沟通、设施联通、贸易畅通、资金融通、民心相通"为主要内容。"一带一路"建设始终秉持开放包容、互利共赢的理念，不是中国一家独奏，而是沿线国家的大合

Joining Hands to Build a Silk Road Economic Belt and a 21st Century Maritime Silk Road – Vision and Actions

At the Boao Forum for Asia on March 28, 2015, a white paper entitled *Joining Hands to Build a Silk Road Economic Belt and a 21st Century Maritime Silk Road – Vision and Actions* was issued by China's National Development and Reform Commission, Ministry of Foreign Affairs, and Ministry of Commerce, with the authorization of the State Council.

The document explains the background of the initiative, and outlines its guiding principles and broad objectives, and the priority areas and mechanisms for cooperation. It emphasizes the need for joint efforts through consultation to bring benefits to all, and calls for policy coordination, infrastructure connectivity, unimpeded trade, financial integration, and closer people-to-people ties. Also highlighted is the inclusive approach to building the Belt and Road, with a focus on finding win-win solutions – achieving success requires collaboration of the countries along the proposed routes rather than a solo performance by China. The white paper goes on to illustrate the specific roles

唱。此外，该白皮书还就中国新疆、福建等相关自治区、省份在“一带一路”建设中的角色定位进行了介绍。这份文件在制定过程中，充分听取了“一带一路”沿线国家和相关国际组织的建议，也吸收了中国国内各界人士的意见，是集聚各方智慧的成果。当然，这份白皮书仅是针对“一带一路”提出了方向性、框架性、意向性的设计，未来中国还将与“一带一路”的相关参与方进一步完善和细化。

that can be played by China’s autonomous regions and provinces like Xinjiang and Fujian in implementing the initiative.

The compilation of this white paper was a participatory process. Comments and suggestions were sought from the countries along the proposed routes and interested international organizations, as well as from various quarters in China.

The document focuses only on the general direction, broad guidelines and objectives of the Belt and Road Initiative. Further details will be discussed by China and its partners.

“五通”

2013年9月7日，习近平主席在哈萨克斯坦纳扎尔巴耶夫大学发表演讲，首次提出加强“政策沟通、道路联通、贸易畅通、货币流通、民心相通”，共同建设“丝绸之路经济带”的战略倡议。2015年3月28日，中国政府在博鳌亚洲论坛2015年年会期间正式发布《推动共建丝绸之路经济带和21世纪海上丝绸之路的愿景与行动》，提出要以“政策沟通、设施联通、贸易畅通、资金融通、民心相通”（简称“五通”）为主要内容，打造“一带一路”沿线国家政治互信、经济融合、文化互容的利益共同体、责任共同体和命运共同体。在“一带一路”建设全面推进过程中，“五通”既相互独立，在不同时间阶段各有重点，也是统一整体，需要相互促进，不可分割。

Five-Pronged Approach

In his speech at Kazakhstan's Nazarbayev University on September 7, 2013, President Xi Jinping proposed building a Silk Road Economic Belt by promoting policy coordination, road connectivity, unimpeded trade, currency convertibility, and closer people-to-people ties.

At the Boao Forum for Asia on March 28, 2015, the Chinese government issued a white paper entitled *Joining Hands to Build a Silk Road Economic Belt and a 21st Century Maritime Silk Road – Vision and Actions*. This document also calls for policy coordination, connectivity of infrastructure and facilities, unimpeded trade, financial integration, and closer people-to-people ties (a five-pronged approach), so as to build a community of shared interests, of shared responsibility and of a shared future on the basis of mutual trust, economic integration and cultural inclusiveness.

While the five components of this approach are distinct from one another and will have a shifting focus at different stages in building the Belt and Road, they form an integrated whole, and are inseparable and mutually reinforcing.

建设目标

Building Blocks

利益共同体

“一带一路”沿线国家的总人口约44亿，经济总量约21万亿美元，分别占世界的63%和29%。受资源禀赋、产业基础、历史条件等因素的制约，各国之间发展不平衡，而且大部分为发展中国家。“一带一路”贯穿欧亚非大陆，东牵发展势头强劲的东亚经济圈，西连发达的欧洲北美经济圈，有望建成世界跨度最大、最具活力的经济走廊，形成沿线国家经济利益对接整合的格局。“一带一路”建设旨在激发沿线各国发挥比较优势，将经济互补性转化为发展推动力。通过沿线国家的互联互通和贸易投资便利化等深度国际经济合作，打造世界经济新的增长极，最终实现互利共赢。

Community of Shared Interests

The countries along the proposed Belt and Road routes – most of which are developing countries – have a combined population of 4.4 billion and an aggregate output of US$21 trillion. These represent 63 percent of the world's population and 29 percent of its economic aggregate. Individual countries each have their own natural resources, infrastructure, and historical experiences; such differences, among other factors, have led to different levels of development.

Spanning three continents – Asia, Europe and Africa – the Belt and Road is expected to become the world's most expansive and most dynamic economic corridor, with vibrant East Asia at one end and the developed economies of Europe and North America at the other. Such integration will contribute to a better alignment of economic interests.

In a joint effort to build the Belt and Road each country's comparative strengths can be better exploited, and economic complementarity can be better transformed into new drivers of development. The initiative will rely on wide-ranging international economic cooperation to promote connectivity and facilitate trade and investment. It envisions a world of new economic growth, where win-win strategies are favored.

责任共同体

“一带一路”倡议由中国提出，但需要沿线国家和相关国家共同参与建设。在推动落实倡议的过程中，相关各方会有不同侧重的利益考虑，也会遇到各种难以预料的问题，这就需要大家集思广益。各国须携手应对面临的挑战，合力化解存在的威胁，共同承担产生的责任。当然，由于各国参与的深度和方式有所不同，承担的责任也不尽相同。中国领导人多次表态，“一带一路”建设不是中国的后花园，而是百花园；不是中国的独奏曲，而是各方的协奏曲。作为倡议方，中国会诚心诚意对待沿线国家，做到言必信、行必果，承担起应尽的责任。

Community of Shared Responsibility

Although the Belt and Road Initiative was proposed by China, participation of other countries along the proposed routes and related countries is indispensable to its implementation. Divergent national interests and priorities, as well as unforeseen events, could present a serious challenge. Broad-based consultation is therefore essential. Only through joint efforts and shared responsibility can any threat to progress be neutralized. From this perspective it is agreed that responsibilities could vary depending on different levels of participation.

The Chinese leadership has repeatedly affirmed that the Belt and Road is an undertaking shared by many, rather than being driven by China alone; and the process of creating such a network is a collaborative undertaking, rather than a solo performance by China.

As a sponsor, China is ready and willing to act in good faith toward its partners, honor its commitments, and fulfill its responsibilities.

命运共同体

在中共十八大报告中，“命运共同体”作为一种促进中国与世界实现合作共赢关系的理念被明确提出。此后，“命运共同体”逐渐成为中国外交的核心理念之一，也是“一带一路”建设的重要目标。“命运共同体”强调整体思维，推崇共生共荣的关系，追求持久和平和共同繁荣。一个国家的命运要掌握在本国人民手中，世界的前途命运必须由各国共同掌握，各国在追求本国利益时兼顾别国利益，在追求自身发展时兼顾别国发展。“一带一路”建设背后体现的正是这种“命运共同体”思想。通过“一带一路”构建命运共同体，需要建立在利益共同体和责任共同体的基础之上。一方面，要在经贸和投资领域不断扩大利益交汇点，把经济的互补性转化为发

Community of Shared Future

The idea of building a community of shared future was first discussed in a report to the 18th CPC National Congress in 2012. It was seen as contributing to China's engagement with the rest of the world in pursuit of win-win results. This idea has since become a core element of China's foreign policy. It also underpins the launch of the Belt and Road Initiative.

The concept of a community of shared future emphasizes the virtue of holistic thinking, cosmopolitan ideals, and the pursuit of lasting peace and shared prosperity. The destiny of a country should be in the hands of its people, and the future of the world must be shaped jointly by the peoples of the world. A country's national interests are to be pursued with other countries' interests in mind. The implementation of any national development strategy should be accompanied by careful consideration of the development needs of others.

Underlying the Belt and Road Initiative is the understanding that we all share one world. Under the Belt and Road Initiative, a community of shared future can be built only on the basis of shared interests and responsibility. Sustained efforts should thus be made to expand our cooperation in the fields of trade and investment, where

展的互助力；另一方面，各国需要共同担负解决国际性难题的责任，共同打造互利共赢的合作架构。

convergence of interests occurs, and to transform economic complementarity into new drivers of development. At the same time, all countries should join hands in dealing with international challenges and building a cooperative framework that benefits all.

绿色丝绸之路

环境问题是人类社会面临的共同问题。2016年6月22日，习近平主席在乌兹别克斯坦最高会议立法院发表演讲时指出，要着力深化环保合作，践行绿色发展理念，加大生态环境保护力度，携手打造绿色丝绸之路。此前中国公布的《推动共建丝绸之路经济带和21世纪海上丝绸之路的愿景与行动》也明确提出，强化基础设施绿色低碳化建设和运营管理，在建设中充分考虑气候变化影响，在投资贸易中突出生态文明理念，加强生态环境、生物多样性和应对气候变化合作，共建绿色丝绸之路。绿色丝绸之路体现了可持续发展的理念，它要求在“一带一路”建设中秉承绿色和环保理念，正确处理经济增长和环境保护的关系，充分考虑沿线国家的生态承

Silk Road of Green Development

Environmental protection is a common concern of humanity. Addressing the Legislative Chamber of the Uzbek Supreme Assembly on June 22, 2016, President Xi Jinping emphasized the need to strengthen cooperation in environmental and ecological protection, so as to build a Silk Road of green development.

This idea had previously been affirmed by the Chinese government in a white paper entitled *Joining Hands to Build a Silk Road Economic Belt and a 21st Century Maritime Silk Road – Vision and Actions*. The document highlights the importance of a green, low-carbon approach to building and operating infrastructure, taking into full account the imperative to mitigate the impact of climate change. It encourages joint efforts to build a Silk Road of green development by integrating ecological considerations into trade and investment strategies, and expanding cooperation in protecting the environment and biodiversity and addressing climate change.

Contributing to the goal of sustainable development, and informed by the concept of environmentally friendly development, the Silk Road of green development initiative calls for a careful balance between economic growth and environmental protection, with

载能力，共建一个良好的生态环境。“一带一路”建设已将生态环保、防沙治沙、清洁能源等列为重点发展产业，绿色丝绸之路面临发展良机。

due consideration given to the ecological carrying capacity of the countries concerned. Ecological protection, prevention and control of desertification, and clean energy, among others, already feature prominently in strategic planning exercises for implementing the Belt and Road Initiative. The prospects for a Silk Road of green development look bright.

健康丝绸之路

推进全球卫生事业，是落实2030年可持续发展议程的重要组成部分。2016年6月22日，习近平主席在乌兹别克斯坦最高会议立法院发表演讲时提议，着力深化医疗卫生合作，加强在传染病疫情通报、疾病防控、医疗救援、传统医药领域互利合作，携手打造健康丝绸之路。2017年1月18日，中国政府与世界卫生组织签署了双方关于“一带一路”卫生领域合作的谅解备忘录。健康丝绸之路的主要目标是提高“一带一路”沿线国家整体的健康卫生水平。主要措施包括：沿线国家加强在卫生体制政策、卫生领域相关国际标准和规范的磋商和沟通，加强重点传染病防控合作，加强人员培训，推动更多中国生产的医药产品进入国际市场，使质优价廉的中国医药产品造福“一带一路”沿线国家人民，等等。

Silk Road of Health Cooperation

Promoting health at a global level is an important component of the 2030 Agenda for Sustainable Development. In his speech to the Legislative Chamber of the Uzbek Supreme Assembly on June 22, 2016, President Xi Jinping proposed expanding cooperation in health under the framework of the Belt and Road Initiative, that is, jointly building a Silk Road of health cooperation, by strengthening information sharing on a range of measures including communicable diseases, disease prevention and control, medical relief and assistance, and exchanges on traditional medical research. On January 18, 2017, the Chinese government and the World Health Organization signed a memorandum of understanding to this end.

A Silk Road of health cooperation aims to improve public health in countries along the Belt and Road. Key measures include increased consultation and exchanges on health policy issues, building institutions, defining international health standards and norms, enhanced cooperation in disease prevention and control, and personnel training and capacity building. Efforts will also be stepped up to facilitate global access to high-quality and affordable China-made pharmaceutical products beneficial to people along the Belt and Road.

智力丝绸之路

推进“一带一路”战略，人才是关键。2016年6月20日，习近平主席在华沙出席丝路国际论坛时提出，智力先行，强化智库的支撑引领作用。加强对“一带一路”建设方案和路径的研究，在规划对接、政策协调、机制设计上做好政府的参谋和助手，在理念传播、政策解读、民意通达上做好桥梁和纽带。两天后的6月22日，他在乌兹别克斯坦最高会议立法院发表演讲时明确提出，中方倡议成立“一带一路”职业技术合作联盟，培养培训各类专业人才，携手打造智力丝绸之路。在“一带一路”建设推进过程中，会面临很多新问题、新挑战，需要越来越多的智力和人才支持，需要各方相互学习、取长补短，共同提出解决方案。当前，“一带一路”沿线国家人才短缺的问题不同程度地存在，智力丝绸之路的主要目标是推进沿线国家人才培养和智力交流。

Silk Road of Innovation

Talent management is key to effectively implementing the Belt and Road Initiative. At the Silk Road Forum in Warsaw on June 20, 2016, President Xi Jinping emphasized the unique role talent development can play in leading the way in this regard. It is important, he pointed out, to promote research on courses of action and means to achieve the goals of the initiative, so as to inform decision-making with regard to strategic planning and alignment, policy coordination, and the design of mechanisms. Also crucial is effective dissemination of information about the guiding principles of the initiative and interpretation of policies so as to better reach out to the people.

Addressing the Legislative Chamber of the Uzbek Supreme Assembly on June 22, 2016, Xi proposed the establishment of a technical cooperation alliance under the Belt and Road Initiative to facilitate personnel training and capacity building.

Any new progress in implementing the initiative will, to be sure, be accompanied by new challenges. Overcoming these challenges requires brainpower and expertise. It is therefore vital for countries to learn from each other and join hands in finding solutions. The objective of a Silk Road of innovation is to enhance talent development and exchange of expertise in response to any shortfall of skilled personnel in countries along the proposed Belt and Road.

和平丝绸之路

“一带一路”沿线，尤其是丝绸之路经济带沿线，面临较为严重的恐怖主义、分裂主义和极端主义威胁，部分国家之间的关系较为紧张，时常伴有局部冲突，也有部分国家内部政局不稳。因此，破解地区动荡局势，维护地区和平稳定，对于“一带一路”建设至关重要。2016年6月22日，习近平主席在乌兹别克斯坦最高会议立法院发表演讲时提出，着力深化安保合作，践行共同、综合、合作、可持续的亚洲安全观，推动构建具有亚洲特色的安全治理模式，携手打造和平丝绸之路。和平丝绸之路包含两个基本内涵：一是“一带一路”建设必须在相对和平的环境里进行；二是“一带一路”建设能促进地区和平稳定。以发展促和平促安全，这是中国提出的思路，也是被实践证明很有成效的办法。

Silk Road of Peace

Serious terrorist, secessionist and extremist threats lurk along the Belt and Road, especially along the Belt. There is also tension between some of the countries along the routes, giving rise to occasional localized conflicts. Furthermore, a number of countries are subject to internal instability. For the Belt and Road plan to proceed, it is crucial to defuse turmoil and maintain peace and stability at the regional level.

In his speech to the Legislative Chamber of the Uzbek Supreme Assembly on June 22, 2016, President Xi Jinping called for enhanced security cooperation. It is critical, he said, to promote a new Asian security concept that emphasizes joint and comprehensive measures and cooperation in ensuring sustainable security, and to create a security governance framework with Asian characteristics – in sum, to jointly build a Silk Road of peace.

A Silk Road of peace rests on two mutually complementary pillars: an environment of relative stability, which is indispensable for the Belt and Road Initiative to thrive; and concerted efforts to build the trade network, which contributes to regional peace and stability. China believes that development promotes peace and security, a conviction that has been borne out by experience.

合作重点

Priority Areas of Cooperation

政策沟通

政策沟通是“一带一路”建设的重要保障。政策沟通的基本含义是：在深化利益融合、促进政治互信并达成合作新共识的前提下，本着求同存异的原则，沿线各国积极构建政府间宏观政策沟通的交流机制，就经济发展战略和对策进行充分交流对接，共同制定推进区域合作的规划和措施，协商解决合作中的问题，共同为务实合作及大型项目实施提供政策支持，从而形成趋向一致的战略、决策、政策和规则，结成更为巩固的命运共同体。

Policy Coordination

Policy coordination is key to effective implementation of the Belt and Road Initiative. In order to expand shared interests, enhance mutual trust, and build consensus on further cooperation, it is important for the countries along the Belt and Road to seek common ground while shelving differences, and increase inter-governmental communication on macroeconomic policies and development strategies so as to better align their national priorities with regional planning needs and common goals. Cooperation-related issues and challenges should be dealt with through consultation, and policy support is needed to promote a pragmatic approach to implementing large-scale projects. Joint efforts have to be made to harmonize strategies, decision-making processes, policies and rules, so as to build a stronger community of shared future.

设施联通

基础设施互联互通是“一带一路”建设的优先领域。在尊重相关国家主权和安全关切的基础上，推动沿线各国加强基础设施建设规划、技术标准体系的对接，共同推进国际骨干通道建设，逐步形成连接亚洲各区域以及亚欧非之间的基础设施网络。在推进设施联通过程中，还特别强调基础设施的绿色低碳化建设和运营管理，充分考虑气候变化影响。它既包括传统的公路、铁路、航空、航运、管道等的联通，也包括电力、电信、邮政、边防、海关和质检、规划等新领域的联通，从而将活跃的东亚经济圈、发达的欧洲经济圈和

Connectivity of Infrastructure

Connectivity of infrastructure is a priority area under the Belt and Road Initiative. While respect for each other's sovereignty and security concerns is indispensable, a closer alignment of infrastructure development planning and technical standards is called for between the countries along the Belt and Road. Such a move would facilitate the construction of key international arteries, so as to build an infrastructure network that not only links all the subregions in Asia, but also extends out to Europe and Africa. Also essential is the need to promote a green and low-carbon approach to building and operating infrastructure, taking into full account the imperative to mitigate the impact of climate change.

Rather than confined to the traditional sense of connection by means of highways, railways, aviation routes, shipping routes and pipelines, the new notion of connectivity is understood to cover such areas as power supplies, telecommunications, postal services, border controls, customs, quality controls, and integrated planning as well. Efforts to boost connectivity aim to link the vibrant East Asia with the developed economies in Western Europe, covering a host of other countries in between with huge potential for economic

经济发展潜力巨大的中间广大腹地国家结成携手发展的利益共同体。

development. With interests interlocked, all countries concerned are encouraged to seek cooperation in pursuit of shared prosperity.

贸易畅通

贸易畅通是“一带一路”建设的重点内容，旨在激发释放沿线国家的合作潜力，做大做好合作“蛋糕”。采取的措施主要包括：沿线国家共同建设自由贸易网络体系，消除投资和贸易壁垒，促进贸易和投资便利化；共同商建自由贸易区，构建区域内和各国良好的营商环境，激发释放合作潜力；共同提高技术性贸易措施透明度，降低非关税壁垒，提高贸易自由化便利化水平；共同拓宽贸易领域，优化贸易结构，挖掘贸易新增长点，促进贸易平衡；把投资和贸易有机结合起来，以投资带动贸易发展，在投资贸易中突出生态文明理念，加强生态环境、生物多样性和应对气候变化合作，共建绿色丝绸之路；共同优化产业链、价值链、供应链和服务链，促进沿线国家和地区产业互补、互动与互助；

Unimpeded Trade

Removing barriers to trade with the aim of unleashing the potential for greater cooperation among countries involved is a major task in building the Belt and Road. Major measures the countries and regions along the Belt and Road could take include:

– creating mechanisms to facilitate free trade and the removal of investment and trade barriers;

– opening free trade areas to create a business-friendly environment at the regional and national levels and unleash the potential for cooperation;

– improving the transparency of technical measures and reducing non-tariff barriers in order to liberalize and facilitate trade;

– expanding trading areas, improving trade structures, and exploring new growth areas in order to attain trade balance;

– integrating investment and trade, and boosting trade with investment; incorporating a focus on cooperation in ecological conservation, protecting bio-diversity and addressing climate change into investment and trade strategies in a joint effort to build a Silk Road of green development;

– optimizing industry, value, supply and service chains, and promoting economic complementarity, interaction and mutual assistance between countries and regions

共同探索新的开放开发之路，形成互利共赢、多元平衡、安全高效的开放型经济体系。

concerned; and

– exploring new development opportunities, and creating an open economic environment that encourages the search for win-win solutions, respects diversity, enhances security and promotes efficiency.

资金融通

资金融通是"一带一路"建设的重要支撑。主要举措包括：沿线国家深化金融合作，推进亚洲货币稳定体系、投融资体系和信用体系建设，通过提供更多惠及各方的公共金融产品，推动金融系统化；共同推进亚洲基础设施投资银行、金砖国家开发银行筹建，加快丝路基金组建运营，发挥丝路基金以及各国主权基金在"一带一路"重点项目建设中的资金引导作用；扩大沿线国家双边本币结算和货币互换的范围和规模，推动亚洲债券市场的开放和发展，支持沿线国家政府和信用等级较高的企业及金融机构在中国境内发行人民币债券，符合条件的中国境内金融机构和企业可以在境外发行人民币债券和外币债券，发挥各国融资作用；深化银行联合体务实合作，以银团贷款、银行授信等方式开展多边金融合作，引导商业股权投资基金和社会资金参与"一带一路"重点项目共建；加强金融监管合作，完善风险应对

Financial Integration

Financial integration is an important support for the Belt and Road Initiative. Key measures the countries concerned could take to foster financial integration include:

– increasing financial cooperation to ensure currency stability, build a sound framework for investment, financing, and credit services in Asia, and expand the availability of public financial products;

– strengthening the role of the Asian Infrastructure Investment Bank, the BRICS New Development Bank, the Silk Road Fund, and sovereign wealth funds of the countries concerned in funding key projects;

– expanding local currency settlement for bilateral trade, and promoting the opening up and development of bond markets in Asia in support of RMB bond issuance in China by governments and creditworthy companies and financial institutions of other Belt and Road countries, and the issuance of bonds denominated in the RMB or foreign currencies outside China by Chinese companies and financial institutions;

– facilitating interbank and multilateral cooperation, especially in issuing syndicated loans and bank credit, and encouraging equity funds, other companies and individuals to invest in key projects; and

– enhancing cooperation on financial regulation, improving risk response and crisis

和危机处置的制度安排，构建区域性金融风险预警系统，形成应对跨境风险和危机处置的交流合作机制，助推经贸合作深化发展。

management mechanisms, and building a regional financial risk early-warning system, to address any cross-border risks and crises and promote further economic and trade cooperation.

民心相通

民心相通是“一带一路”建设的社会根基。作为一项沟通多元文化和众多国家的重大战略构想，“一带一路”能否成功，从根本上取决于民心能否相通，直接体现在沿线国家人民的获得感、认可度和参与度上。为此，沿线各国要传承和弘扬丝绸之路友好合作精神，广泛开展文化交流、学术往来、人才交流、媒体合作、科技合作、青年和妇女交往、志愿者服务等领域的务实合作，增进相互了解和传统友谊，为深化双边和多边合作奠定坚实的民意基础。具体措施包括：加强沿线国家民间组织的交流合作，充分发挥政党、议会交往的桥梁作用，推动沿线国家智库之间开展联合研究、合作举办论坛，加强文化传媒的国际交流合作，促进不同文明和宗教之间的交流对话，等等。

Closer People-to-People Ties

People-to-people ties provide an anchor for the Belt and Road Initiative. Without such an anchor, the strategic goal of connecting diverse cultures and different countries would be out of reach. Increased interaction and mutual understanding, greater awareness of potential benefits from expanded cooperation, and more participation are therefore indispensable to the initiative's success.

To this end, the countries along the Belt and Road are encouraged to step up friendly cooperation in the Silk Road tradition by promoting extensive cultural, academic, scientific, media, and other people-to-people exchanges, including those between youths, women, and volunteer groups, so as to consolidate public support for bilateral and multilateral cooperation.

Specific measures include: expanding exchanges among non-governmental organizations; strengthening the role of political parties and parliaments in promoting bilateral and multilateral interaction; encouraging collaboration among think tanks in conducting research and sponsoring forums on issues of common concern; and fostering dialogues among civilizations and religions through increased exchanges between cultural and media organizations.

『走廊』建设

Economic Corridors

中蒙俄经济走廊

2014年9月11日，习近平主席在塔吉克斯坦首都杜尚别举行的首次中蒙俄三国元首会晤期间，提出打造中蒙俄经济走廊的倡议，获得普京总统和额勒贝格道尔吉总统的积极响应。2016年6月23日，三国正式签署《建设中蒙俄经济走廊规划纲要》，这是“一带一路”倡议下的第一个多边合作规划纲要。中蒙俄经济走廊是丝绸之路经济带的重要组成部分，旨在推动“一带一路”倡议同俄罗斯的“欧亚联盟”倡议、蒙古国的“草原之路”倡议实现对接，为三国深化务实合作搭建顶层设计平台，以便发挥三方的潜力和优势，建设和拓展互利共赢的经济发展空间，推动地区经济一体化，提升三国在国际市场上的联合竞争力。中蒙俄经济走廊有两个通道：一是从华北的京津冀到呼和浩特，再到蒙古和俄罗斯；二是从大连、沈阳、长春、哈尔滨到满洲里和俄罗斯的赤塔。该走廊重点关

China-Mongolia-Russia Economic Corridor

The idea of the China-Mongolia-Russia Economic Corridor (CMREC) was proposed by President Xi Jinping on September 11, 2014 during the first trilateral meeting of the three heads of state in Dushanbe, capital of Tajikistan, and was welcomed by Russian President Vladimir Putin and the then Mongolian President Tsakhiagiin Elbegdorj. On June 23, 2016, the three countries put pen to paper on a development plan for the proposal, the first multilateral cooperation plan to form part of the Belt and Road Initiative.

As an important component of the Silk Road Economic Belt, the CMREC aims to align China's Belt and Road Initiative with Russia's proposal for the Eurasian Union and Mongolia's Steppe Road program. It is expected to create an overarching platform to tap the potential and strengths of the three parties to expand development opportunities beneficial to all, promote regional economic integration, and enhance their collective competitiveness in the international market.

The CMREC has two key traffic arteries: one extends from China's Beijing-Tianjin-Hebei region to Hohhot and on to Mongolia and Russia; the other extends from China's Dalian, Shenyang, Changchun, Harbin and Manzhouli to Russia's Chita.

注七大合作领域，即促进交通基础设施发展及互联互通、加强口岸建设和海关及检验检疫监管、加强产能与投资合作、深化经贸合作、拓展人文交流合作、加强生态环保合作、推动地方及边境地区合作，其中交通领域被确定为工作重点。

Seven major areas of cooperation are envisaged: transport infrastructure and connectivity; port construction, and customs and border inspection and quarantine services; industrial capacity and investment; trade; cultural and people-to-people exchanges; environmental protection; and cooperation with adjacent regions. Transport is the main focus.

新亚欧大陆桥

新亚欧大陆桥是相对“西伯利亚大陆桥”（从俄罗斯东部沿海的符拉迪沃斯托克出发，横穿西伯利亚大铁路通向莫斯科，然后通向欧洲各国）而言的，又名“第二亚欧大陆桥”，东起江苏连云港、山东日照等中国沿海港口城市，西至荷兰鹿特丹、比利时安特卫普等欧洲口岸，途经哈萨克斯坦、俄罗斯、白俄罗斯、波兰、德国等，全长约10800千米，辐射世界30多个国家和地区，是横跨亚欧两大洲、连接太平洋和大西洋的国际大通道。20世纪90年代初，新亚欧大陆桥初步开通。“一带一路”有力推动了新亚欧大陆桥建设，为沿线国家和亚欧两大洲经济贸易交流提供了便捷的大通道。作为“一带一路”建设的标志性项目，渝新欧、蓉新欧、义新欧等多条铁路运输干线已经开通，其中渝新欧从重庆出发，通过位于中东欧的波兰抵达德国的杜伊斯堡，蓉新欧则是从成都出发，直接抵达波兰，义新欧则从浙江义乌出发，抵达西班牙首都马德里。与此同时，与新亚欧大陆桥建设相关的公路交通、输电线路、港口建设等方面的工作也在稳步推进。

New Eurasian Land Bridge

The New Eurasian Land Bridge (NELB) is an international passageway linking the Pacific and the Atlantic. As distinct from the Siberian Landbridge, which goes from Russia's eastern port of Vladivostok through Siberia to Moscow and onward to West European countries, this "second" bridge goes from China's coastal cities of Lianyungang and Rizhao to Holland's Rotterdam and Belgium's Antwerp. The 10,800-kilometer-long rail link runs through Kazakhstan, Russia, Belarus, Poland and Germany, and serves more than 30 countries and regions.

Opened in the early 1990s, the NELB is gaining new impetus from the Belt and Road Initiative. It greatly facilitates trade and other exchanges among the countries along the route and between Asia and Europe.

To date, several transcontinental rail routes, which showcase the potential of the Belt and Road Initiative, have entered service. These include the Chongqing-Xinjiang-Europe Railway (reaching Germany's Duisburg via Poland), the Chengdu-Xinjiang-Europe Railway (reaching Poland), and the Yiwu-Xinjiang-Europe Railway (reaching Madrid). The construction of associated highways, power transmission lines, and ports is progressing in a steady manner.

中国—中亚—西亚经济走廊

中国—中亚—西亚经济走廊东起中国，向西至阿拉伯半岛，是中国与中亚和西亚各国之间形成的一个经济合作区域，大致与古丝绸之路范围相吻合。走廊从新疆出发，穿越中亚地区，抵达波斯湾、地中海沿岸和阿拉伯半岛，主要涉及中亚五国（哈萨克斯坦、吉尔吉斯斯坦、塔吉克斯坦、乌兹别克斯坦、土库曼斯坦）和西亚的伊朗、沙特阿拉伯、土耳其等17个国家和地区，是丝绸之路经济带的重要组成部分。尽管中亚、西亚地区资源丰富，但制约经济社会发展的因素很多，其中基础设施建设落后、缺乏资金技术等问题较为突出。通过中国—中亚—西亚经济走廊建设，打通该地区对外经贸合作和资金流动通道，有利于促进相关国家经济社会发展。

China-Central Asia-West Asia Economic Corridor

The China-Central Asia-West Asia Economic Corridor (CCWAEC) links China and the Arabian Peninsula. The vast region it covers generally follows the trajectory of the ancient Silk Road.

The corridor starts from China's Xinjiang and traverses Central Asia before reaching the Persian Gulf, the Mediterranean Sea and the Arabian Peninsula. It crosses five Central Asian countries (Kazakhstan, Kyrgyzstan, Tajikistan, Uzbekistan and Turkmenistan) and 17 countries and regions in West Asia (including Iran, Saudi Arabia and Turkey). It is an important component of the Silk Road Economic Belt.

Central and West Asia are rich in resources, but many factors – backward infrastructure and lack of funds in particular – hinder local development. The CCWAEC will facilitate economic and trade cooperation and flow of capital to these regions, boosting local economic and social development.

中国—中南半岛经济走廊

中南半岛与中国陆海相连，有几千年的历史渊源，有很强的地缘、人缘和文缘关系，是联通“一带一路”的重要桥梁和纽带。中国—中南半岛经济走廊东起珠三角经济区，沿南广高速公路、南广高速铁路，经南宁、凭祥、河内至新加坡，纵贯中南半岛的越南、老挝、柬埔寨、泰国、缅甸、马来西亚等国家，是中国连接中南半岛的大陆桥，也是中国与东盟合作的跨国经济走廊。该走廊以沿线中心城市为依托，以铁路、公路为载体和纽带，以人员、物资、资金、信息的流通为基础，开拓新的战略通道和空间，加快形成优势互补、区域分工、共同发展的区域经济体。携手共建中国—中南半岛经济走廊有利于打造新的区域增长点，促进中南半岛沿线国家的共同繁荣发展，也有利于构建中国—东盟命运共同体。

China-Indochina Peninsula Economic Corridor

China and the Indochina Peninsula are connected by land and sea, with close geographical, cultural, and people-to-people ties. The Indochina Peninsula is an important link on the Belt and Road.

The China-Indochina Peninsula Economic Corridor (CICPEC) extends from China's Pearl River Delta westward along the Nanchong-Guang'an Expressway and the Nanning-Guangzhou High-speed Railway via Nanning and Pingxiang to Hanoi and Singapore.

This land bridge links China with the Indochina Peninsula and crosses the heart of Vietnam, Laos, Cambodia, Thailand, Myanmar and Malaysia. It is expected to boost China's cooperation with the ASEAN countries.

The CICPEC project aims to better connect cities in this region with a network of railways and highways to facilitate the flow of people, goods, capital and information. It will open up new opportunities for strategic cooperation, and create a regional economy bolstered by complementary strengths to ensure sound regional development. By creating new regional growth drivers, it will help achieve common prosperity on the peninsula, and strengthen the China-ASEAN community of shared future.

中巴经济走廊

中巴经济走廊是李克强总理于2013年5月访问巴基斯坦时提出的。走廊起点位于新疆喀什，终点在巴基斯坦瓜达尔港，全长3000千米，北接丝绸之路经济带，南连21世纪海上丝绸之路，是贯通南北丝路的关键枢纽，是一条包括公路、铁路、油气管道和光缆覆盖的“四位一体”通道和贸易走廊，被称为“一带一路”的“旗舰项目”。2015年4月，中巴两国初步制定了中巴经济走廊远景规划，将在走廊沿线建设交通运输和电力设施，并以此带动双方在走廊沿线开展重大项目、基础设施、能源资源、农业水利、信息通讯等多个领域的合作，创立更多工业园区和自贸区。走廊建设预计总工程费将达到450亿美元，计划于2030年完工。2015年4月20日，习近平主席和纳瓦兹•谢里夫总理举行了走廊五大项目破土动工仪式，并签订了超过30项涉及中巴经济走廊的合作协议和备忘录。走廊旨在进一步加强中巴之间交通、能源、海

China-Pakistan Economic Corridor

The China-Pakistan Economic Corridor (CPEC) was proposed by Premier Li Keqiang during a visit to Pakistan in May 2013.

The 3,000-kilometer-long corridor starts from China's Kashi and ends at Pakistan's Gwadar, and connects the Silk Road Economic Belt in the north and the 21st Century Maritime Silk Road in the south. It is a trade network of highways, railways, pipelines and optical cables, and a flagship project under the Belt and Road Initiative.

China and Pakistan developed a long-term plan for the construction of transport and power facilities along the corridor in April 2015. These facilities are expected to spur the launch of other major projects in infrastructure, energy, water conservancy, and information and communications, including industrial parks and free trade zones. With an investment totaling US$45 billion, construction of the CPEC is scheduled to be completed by 2030.

President Xi Jinping and the then Prime Minister Nawaz Sharif were present at the ground-breaking ceremony for five major projects on April 20, 2015, when over 30 agreements and memoranda in relation to CPEC cooperation were signed.

The CPEC is designed to enhance bilateral exchanges and cooperation in

洋等领域的交流与合作，推动互联互通建设，促进两国共同发展。走廊也有助于促进整个南亚的互联互通，更能使南亚、中亚、北非、海湾国家等通过经济、能源领域的合作紧密联合起来，形成惠及近30亿人口的经济共同振兴。

transport, energy and maritime shipping, foster connectivity between the two countries, and promote common development. It will also help enhance connectivity across South Asia, and expand cooperation in economic and energy sectors between the countries in South and Central Asia, North Africa and along the Persian Gulf, thus forming an economic radius benefiting nearly 3 billion people.

孟中印缅经济走廊

2013年5月，李克强总理访问印度期间，中印两国共同倡议建设孟中印缅经济走廊，推动中印两个大市场更紧密连接，加强该地区互联互通。该倡议得到孟加拉国、缅甸两国的积极响应。2013年12月，孟中印缅经济走廊联合研究工作组第一次会议在昆明召开，各方签署了孟中印缅经济走廊联合研究计划，正式建立了四国政府推进孟中印缅合作的机制。2014年9月，习近平主席在访问印度期间同莫迪总理会谈时提出中印双方要加快推进孟中印缅经济走廊建设，开展在“一带一路”框架内的合作。2014年12月，在孟加拉国考斯巴萨举行了孟中印缅经济走廊联合研究工作组第二次会议，讨论并展望了经济走廊的前景、优先次序和发展方向。2017年4月，

Bangladesh-China-India-Myanmar Economic Corridor

The proposal for the Bangladesh-China-India-Myanmar Economic Corridor (BCIMEC) was unveiled by China and India during Premier Li Keqiang's visit to India in May 2013, with the objective of linking the two huge markets of China and India and enhancing regional connectivity. Bangladesh and Myanmar welcomed the proposal.

In December 2013, the first BCIMEC joint study group meeting was held in Kunming, and a joint study plan was signed by all parties, leading to the establishment of a mechanism for cooperation among the four governments.

When meeting with Prime Minister Narendra Modi in India in September 2014, President Xi Jinping suggested that China and India spearhead a joint effort to accelerate the construction of the BCIMEC under the framework of the Belt and Road Initiative.

At its second meeting in Cox's Bazar, Bangladesh in December 2014, the BCIMEC joint study group discussed the vision, priorities, and direction of future development of the BCIMEC.

In April 2017, the BCIMEC joint study group met for the third time in India's Kolkata, and discussed the research report

孟中印缅经济走廊联合研究工作组第三次会议在印度加尔各答召开，四方代表就四国联合编制的研究报告进行了讨论。四国代表均认为，联合研究报告在互联互通、能源、投融资、货物与服务贸易及投资便利化、可持续发展与人文交流等重点领域的交流与合作达成了诸多共识。孟中印缅经济走廊不仅直接惠及四国，其辐射作用将有助于带动南亚、东南亚、东亚三大经济板块联合发展。

that had been jointly compiled by the four countries. The parties agreed that the report reflected their consensus on exchanges and cooperation in a number of key sectors including connectivity, energy, investment and financing, facilitation of trade and investment in goods and services, sustainable development, and cultural and people-to-people exchanges.

In addition to direct benefits to the four countries, the BCIMEC is expected to boost the integrated development of the three economic plates of South, Southeast and East Asia.

合作机制

Cooperation Mechanisms

“一带一路”国际合作高峰论坛

“一带一路”国际合作高峰论坛是“一带一路”提出以来最高规格的论坛活动，主要包括开幕式、圆桌峰会和高级别会议3个部分。第一届“一带一路”国际合作高峰论坛于2017年5月14日至15日在北京举行，是2017年中国重要的主场外交活动，对推动国际和地区合作具有重要意义。29位外国元首、政府首脑及联合国秘书长、红十字国际委员会主席等3位重要国际组织负责人出席高峰论坛，来自130多个国家的约1500名各界贵宾作为正式代表出席论坛，来自全球的4000余名记者注册报道此次论坛。2017年5月14日，中国国家主席习近平出席论坛开幕式，并发表主旨演讲。经过梳理和汇总形成的高峰论坛成果清单主要涵盖政策沟通、设施联通、贸易畅通、资金融通、民心相通5大类，共76大项270多项具体成果。

2017年5月15日，习近平主持圆桌峰会，并宣布中国将于2019年举办第二届“一带一路”国际合作高峰论坛。

Belt and Road Forum for International Cooperation

This is the highest-level international event organized under the framework of the Belt and Road Initiative. The main events include an opening ceremony, a Leaders Roundtable Summit and a high-level conference.

The first forum was organized by China in Beijing on May 14-15, 2017. A major diplomatic gathering in 2017, it was significant to international and regional cooperation. Twenty-nine foreign heads of state and government attended the forum along with the UN Secretary-General and heads of two other international organizations, in addition to about 1,500 representatives from over 130 countries. About 4,000 global journalists reported the event. Xi Jinping delivered a keynote speech at the opening of the forum.

The major deliverables include more than 270 concrete results in five key areas – policy, infrastructure, trade, finance, and people-to-people connectivity.

Xi Jinping announced on May 15 at the Leaders Roundtable Summit that China would host the forum again in 2019.

上海合作组织

上海合作组织（简称“上合组织”）是由中国、俄罗斯、哈萨克斯坦、吉尔吉斯斯坦、塔吉克斯坦、乌兹别克斯坦于2001年6月15日在上海宣布成立的永久性政府间国际组织。上合组织旨在加强成员国间的友好与信任，鼓励成员国在政治、经贸、文化等领域的有效合作，致力于共同维护地区和平与稳定，推动建立公正合理的国际政治经济新秩序。上合组织对内遵循“互信、互利、平等、协商，尊重多样文明、谋求共同发展”的“上海精神”，对外奉行不结盟、不针对其他国家和地区及开放原则。上合组织最高决策机构是成员国元首理事会，该会议每年举行一次，决定本组织所有重要问题。政府首脑理事会每年举行一次，讨论本组织框架下多边合作和优先领域的战略。上合组织有两个常设机构，分别是设在北京的上合组织秘书处和设在塔什干的上合组织地区反恐怖机构执行委员会。除6个成员国外，目前上合组织还包括阿富汗、白俄罗斯、印度、伊朗、蒙古、巴基斯坦6个观察员国，以及阿塞拜疆、亚美尼亚、柬埔寨、尼泊尔、土

Shanghai Cooperation Organization

The Shanghai Cooperation Organization (SCO) is an inter-governmental organization comprising China, Russia, Kazakhstan, Kyrgyzstan, Tajikistan and Uzbekistan founded in Shanghai on June 15, 2001.

The SCO's mission is to build friendship and trust among member states, encourage effective cooperation in political, economic, trade, cultural and other areas, safeguard regional peace and stability, and promote a new international political and economic order that is fair and rational.

Between themselves the SCO members have developed the "Shanghai Spirit," which is based on mutual trust, mutual benefit, equality, consultation, respect for cultural diversity, and pursuit of common prosperity. Externally they follow the principle of openness and non-alignment, and their strategies and policies are not directed against any third party or any other region.

The top decision-making body of the SCO is the Council of Heads of State, which meets once a year to decide on major issues. Its Council of Heads of Government also meets once a year to discuss priorities and issues of multilateral cooperation. Its two permanent bodies are: the Secretariat in Beijing (China) and the Regional Anti-Terrorist Structure in Tashkent (Uzbekistan).

耳其、斯里兰卡6个对话伙伴。2018年6月9日至10日，上海合作组织成员国元首理事会第十八次会议在山东省青岛市举行，中国国家主席习近平主持会议并出席相关活动。青岛峰会上，各方一致同意要为构建命运共同体加强各方面合作，并在组织发展、安全合作、经济合作、人文合作、对外交往等领域取得重要成果。

Six states have observer status with the SCO: Afghanistan, Belarus, India, Iran, Mongolia and Pakistan; and there are six dialogue partners: Armenia, Azerbaijan, Cambodia, Nepal, Sri Lanka and Turkey.

The Council of Heads of State held its 18th meeting in China's Qingdao on June 9-10, 2018. President Xi Jinping chaired the meeting and attended several activities. The participants agreed to reinforce cooperation to build a global community of shared future, and achieve important progress regarding organization development, security, economic, cultural and humanitarian cooperation, and foreign relations.

中国—东盟“10+1”机制

中国—东盟“10+1”机制是中国与东南亚国家联盟建立的合作机制，自1997年成立以来，双方合作不断扩大与深化，现已发展成一个密切的政治、经济合作组织，成为东亚区域合作的主要机制之一。1991年，中国与东盟开启对话进程，中国成为东盟的对话伙伴国。1997年，双方举行第一次“10+1”领导人会议，宣布建立中国—东盟睦邻互信伙伴关系。2010年1月，中国—东盟自贸区正式建成，这是双方关系史上的重大事件，开启了中国与东盟实现经济一体化的进程。自此，中国成为第一个加入《东南亚友好合作条约》和第一个同东盟建立战略伙伴关系的域外大国，也是第一个同东盟建成自贸区的大国。为保障双方合作的顺利与成效，“10+1”机制确立了一套完整的对话与合作平台，主要包括政府首脑会议、部长级会议和工作组会议。中国—东盟中心是推进双方合作的重要常设机构。

China-ASEAN (10+1) Cooperation Mechanism

Established in 1997, the China-ASEAN (10+1) Cooperation Mechanism has played an important role in promoting closer political and economic ties between China and ASEAN members, and has become one of the major forums for regional cooperation.

China-ASEAN dialogue was launched in 1991. The first China-ASEAN (10+1) summit was convened in 1997 and announced the formation of the China-ASEAN partnership of good-neighborliness and mutual trust. The China-ASEAN Free Trade Area was created in January 2010, representing a milestone in China-ASEAN bilateral relations and initiating the process of China-ASEAN economic integration. China was the first non-ASEAN country to join the Treaty of Amity and Cooperation in Southeast Asia and establish a strategic partnership with ASEAN, and the first major country to build a free trade area with ASEAN.

Necessary platforms for dialogue have been in place to ensure successful and effective bilateral cooperation, including the ASEAN-China Summit, ministerial meetings, and working group meetings. The ASEAN-China Center is a permanent body for promoting bilateral cooperation.

亚太经济合作组织

亚太经济合作组织是亚太地区层级最高、领域最广、最具影响力的经济合作机制。1989年11月，澳大利亚、美国、日本、韩国、新西兰、加拿大及当时的东盟六国在澳大利亚首都堪培拉举行亚太经济合作组织首届部长级会议，标志着亚太经合组织的正式成立。1991年11月，中国正式加入亚太经合组织。亚太经合组织共有21个成员，以及东盟秘书处、太平洋经济合作理事会、太平洋岛国论坛秘书处3个观察员。作为经济论坛，亚太经合组织主要讨论与全球和区域经济有关的议题，如贸易和投资自由化、区域经济一体化、互联互通、经济结构改革和创新发展、全球多边贸易体系、经济技术合作和能力建设等，旨在维护本地区成员的共同利益，促进成员间的经济相互依存，加强开放的多边贸易体制，减少区域贸易和投资壁垒。

Asia-Pacific Economic Cooperation

The Asia-Pacific Economic Cooperation (APEC) forum is the highest-level mechanism for economic cooperation in the Asia-Pacific region.

The forum was formally established in November 1989 at a ministerial meeting in the Australian capital of Canberra, attended by Australia, the US, Japan, South Korea, New Zealand, Canada, and the then six ASEAN countries. China became an APEC member in November 1991.

With 21 member economies and three observers – ASEAN Secretariat, Pacific Economic Cooperation Council, and Pacific Islands Forum – it covers an extensive part of the world and wields significant influence.

As an economic forum, APEC focuses on global and regional economic issues such as trade and investment liberalization, regional economic integration, connectivity, economic structural reform and innovative development, global multilateral trade systems, economic and technological cooperation, and capacity building. Its primary goal is to safeguard the common interests of its member economies in the Asia-Pacific, increase their economic interdependence, create an open multilateral trade system, and reduce regional trade and investment barriers.

亚太经合组织共有5个层次的运作机制：领导人非正式会议、部长级会议、高官会、委员会和工作组、秘书处。中国于2001年和2014年先后在上海和北京成功举办过两届亚太经合组织领导人非正式会议，为促进区域贸易和投资自由化便利化、推动全球和地区经济增长发挥了积极作用。

APEC operates at five institutional levels: meetings of economic leaders, ministerial meetings, meetings of senior officials, committees and working groups, and the Secretariat. China hosted the 2001 and 2014 APEC economic leaders meetings in Shanghai and in Beijing respectively, and has played an active role in promoting free and open regional trade and investment and stimulating regional and global economic growth.

亚欧会议

亚欧会议是亚洲和欧洲间重要的跨区域政府间论坛，旨在促进两大洲间建立新型、全面伙伴关系，加强相互对话、了解与合作，为亚欧经济社会发展创造有利条件。1996年3月，首届亚欧首脑会议在泰国曼谷举行，会议通过了《主席声明》，确定每两年召开一次首脑会议。2014年在意大利米兰举行的第十届亚欧首脑会议，决定接纳克罗地亚和哈萨克斯坦为新成员，亚欧会议成员增至53个。亚欧会议包括政治对话、经贸合作、社会文化及其他领域交流三大支柱，活动机制包括首脑会议、外长会议及部长级会议等，日常工作通过高官会进行沟通协调。亚欧首脑会议负责确定亚欧会议的指导原则和发展方向，隔年在亚洲和欧洲轮流举行，迄今已举办12届。亚欧外长会议负责亚欧会议活动的整体协调和政策规划，通过有关指导性文件

Asia-Europe Meeting

The Asia-Europe Meeting (ASEM) is a major inter-governmental process designed to foster a new comprehensive partnership between Asia and Europe. Its goals are to encourage dialogue, mutual understanding, and cooperation, and create favorable conditions for economic and social development on the two continents.

The First ASEM Summit was held in Bangkok, Thailand, in March 1996. It published a Chairman's Statement and announced the decision to hold a summit of Heads of State and Government every two years. The 10th ASEM Summit, in Milan (Italy) in 2014, accepted Croatia and Kazakhstan as partners, and the number of countries involved rose to 53.

The ASEM rests on three pillars: political dialogue, economic cooperation, and socio-cultural exchanges. Its main activities include the Summits, Foreign Ministers Meetings and other Ministerial Meetings. Its day-to-day operations are coordinated through ASEM Senior Officials Meetings.

The Summits set ASEM principles and priorities. These biennial meetings are held alternately in Asia and Europe, and to date 12 Summits have been convened. The Foreign Ministers Meetings are responsible for the overall coordination and policy planning of all activities, adopting guidance documents and

并批准新倡议。亚欧高官会议负责协调和管理亚欧会议各领域活动，并对首脑会议、外长会议预做准备。成立于1997年的亚欧基金是亚欧会议框架下唯一常设机构，负责开展亚欧学术、文化和人员交流活动。

approving new initiatives.

The Senior Officials Meetings are held to ensure continuity in the work of ASEM and oversee preparations for the Summits and for Foreign Ministers Meetings.

The Asia-Europe Foundation (ASEF), founded in 1997, is the only permanent institution under ASEM. It is tasked with promoting greater mutual understanding between Asia and Europe through academic, cultural and people-to-people exchanges.

亚洲合作对话

亚洲合作对话是目前唯一面向全亚洲的官方对话与合作机制，成立于2002年，旨在推动各成员之间农业、能源、扶贫等领域的交流与合作，通过开展亚洲对话推动亚洲合作、促进亚洲发展。亚洲合作对话机制以首脑会议、外长会议、领域牵头国、高级研究小组会等形式开展活动，目前已在各成员国召开了2次首脑会议和15次外长会议。中国高度重视并积极参与亚洲合作对话进程，支持全面加强亚洲合作对话机制能力建设，更好地服务于亚洲地区发展和一体化进程。近年来，中国先后主办“丝绸之路务实合作论坛”“共建‘一带一路’合作论坛暨亚洲工商大会”等活动，以实际行动助推该对话机制，深化务实合作。

Asia Cooperation Dialogue

The Asia Cooperation Dialogue (ACD) is the only mechanism for official dialogue and cooperation covering the whole of Asia. Inaugurated in 2002, it aims to promote exchanges in areas such as agriculture, energy and poverty reduction, and boost Asia-wide cooperation and development through dialogue.

ACD activities are conducted through its Summits, Foreign Ministers Meetings, prime movers in specific areas, and meetings of high-level study groups. To date, two ACD Summits and 15 Foreign Ministers Meetings have been convened.

Attaching great importance to the dialogue, China is an active participant in ACD activities and supports strengthening the ACD to better serve Asia-wide development and integration. To this end, it has hosted events such as the ACD Forum on Silk Road Cooperation, the ACD Forum on Belt and Road Cooperation and the Asia Business Conference.

亚信会议

亚信会议全称为亚洲相互协作与信任措施会议。1992年10月，哈萨克斯坦总统纳扎尔巴耶夫在第四十七届联合国大会上提出了建立一个全亚洲范围的地区性安全合作组织的倡议，旨在通过各国专家、学者和领导人之间“讨论亚洲或欧亚的和平与安全问题”，促进亚洲各国间的对话和协商。经过长达10年的专家论证和外交协调，2002年6月，亚信会议第一次峰会在阿拉木图成功举行。亚信会议恪守《联合国宪章》的宗旨和原则，坚持各成员国一律平等，相互尊重主权和领土完整，互不干涉内政，倡导以和平方式解决争端，反对动辄诉诸武力或以武力相威胁，通过制定和实施军事政治、新威胁新挑战、经济、人文、生态等五大领域信任措施，加强成员国安全、经济、社会和文化的交流与合

Conference on Interaction and Confidence-Building Measures in Asia

The idea of establishing an Asia-wide forum on security cooperation was first proposed by President Nazarbayev of Kazakhstan in October 1992 at the 47th Session of the UN General Assembly. This regional forum aims to promote dialogue and consultation on Asian or Eurasian peace and security issues among experts, academics and political leaders.

After 10 years of deliberation and diplomatic coordination, the first summit of the Conference on Interaction and Confidence-Building Measures in Asia (CICA) was held in Almaty (Kazakhstan) in June 2002.

The CICA is committed to the purposes and principles of the Charter of the United Nations, including equality of its member states, respect for each other's sovereignty and territorial integrity, non-interference in each other's internal affairs, peaceful settlement of disputes, and the obligation to refrain from the threat or use of force. It encourages exchanges and cooperation among member states on security, economic, social and cultural issues, through the implementation of confidence-building measures to address military, political,

作。亚信会议建立了国家元首和政府首脑会议、外长会议、高官委员会会议、特别工作组会议等议事和决策机制。截止到2014年的上海亚信峰会，亚信会议已有26个成员国，横跨亚洲各区域。在本次峰会上，习近平主席提出了“共同、综合、合作、可持续”的亚洲安全观，倡议走出一条共建、共享、共赢的亚洲安全之路。中国自2014年5月担任，2016年连任亚信会议主席国以来，推动亚信进程取得一系列新的进展，亚信安全合作理念进一步丰富，互信协作共识进一步凝聚，信任措施水平进一步提高，伙伴关系网络进一步拓展。在各方积极参与下，亚信合作潜力得到释放，整体合作逐步走向深入，在国际和地区事务中的参与度和能见度显著提高，已经成为亚洲覆盖范围最广、成员数量最多、代表性最强的安全合作论坛，为促进地区稳定繁荣发挥着重要作用。

economic, cultural and environmental challenges and new threats.

CICA deliberation and decision-making mechanisms include: Meetings of Heads of State and Government, Meetings of Foreign Ministers, the Senior Officials Committee, and the Special Working Group.

The number of CICA member states increased to 26 at the 2014 Shanghai Summit. At that summit, President Xi Jinping introduced an Asian security concept that emphasizes joint and comprehensive measures and cooperation in ensuring sustainable security, one that aims at carving a path through joint efforts to a secure future in the region enjoyed by all.

China assumed the CICA presidency in May 2014 and renewed its term in 2016. Since then it has promoted the CICA process: the CICA philosophy on security cooperation has been enriched, mutual trust and interaction have been enhanced, confidence-building measures have been improved, and the partnership network has been expanded.

The active participation of all parties has unlocked CICA cooperation potential and enhanced overall cooperation, with increasing participation and visibility in international and regional affairs. The CICA is the security cooperation forum with the widest coverage, the largest membership and the broadest representation in Asia, and it now plays an important role in promoting regional stability and prosperity.

中阿合作论坛

2004年1月30日，时任中国国家主席胡锦涛访问了阿拉伯国家联盟总部，会见了时任阿盟秘书长阿姆鲁•穆萨和22个阿盟成员国代表。会见结束后，时任中国外长李肇星与穆萨秘书长共同宣布成立“中国—阿拉伯国家合作论坛”。2014年6月5日，习近平主席在中阿合作论坛第六届部长级会议开幕式上讲话表示，中阿合作论坛是着眼中阿关系长远发展作出的战略抉择，已成为丰富中阿关系战略内涵、推进中阿务实合作的有效抓手。2016年5月12日，中阿合作论坛第七届部长级会议在卡塔尔多哈举行。习近平主席和卡塔尔埃米尔塔米姆•本•哈马德•阿勒萨尼分别致贺信。会议围绕“共建‘一带一路’，深化中阿战略合作”议题，就中阿关系发展和中阿合作论坛建设达成广泛共识。2018年7月10日，中阿合作论坛第八届部长级会议在北京举行。习近平主席出席会议开幕式并发表题为《携手推进新时代中阿战略伙伴关系》的重要

China-Arab States Cooperation Forum

The launch of the China-Arab States Cooperation Forum (CASCF) was announced by the then Foreign Minister Li Zhaoxing of China and the then Secretary-General Amr Moussa of the League of Arab States on January 30, 2004 after the then Chinese President Hu Jintao visited the headquarters of the League, and met with the then Secretary-General Amr Moussa and representatives of this 22-member organization.

Addressing the opening ceremony of the Sixth CASCF Ministerial Meeting on June 5, 2014, Chinese President Xi Jinping characterized the CASCF as of strategic importance for the long-term development of bilateral relations and substantive cooperation.

The Seventh CASCF Ministerial Meeting was held in Doha, capital of Qatar, on May 12, 2016. President Xi Jinping and Qatar Emir Sheikh Tamim bin Hamad Al Thani each sent a letter of congratulations to the meeting. Under the theme of "Jointly Building the Belt and Road to Reinforce Strategic Cooperation," the meeting reached a broad consensus on bilateral relations and future work of the CASCF.

The Eighth CASCF Ministerial Meeting was held in Beijing on July 10, 2018. President Xi Jinping delivered a speech

讲话，宣布中阿双方建立全面合作、共同发展、面向未来的中阿战略伙伴关系。截至2018年7月，中国—阿拉伯国家合作论坛已举行8届部长级会议、15次高官会，并召开了4次中阿高官级战略政治对话。

entitled "Joining Hands to Advance Sino-Arab Strategic Partnership in the New Era" at the opening session. He declared that the two sides had agreed to establish a future-oriented Sino-Arab strategic partnership of comprehensive cooperation and common development.

By July 2018, eight CASCF ministerial meetings and 15 senior officials' meetings had been held, in addition to four strategic and political dialogues at senior official level.

中国—海合会战略对话

2010年6月，中国—海湾合作委员会首轮战略对话在北京举行，时任科威特副首相兼外交大臣穆罕默德、阿联酋外交国务部长卡尔卡什、海合会秘书长阿提亚与杨洁篪外长共同主持了对话会，并签署了双方关于高级别战略对话的谅解备忘录。2011年5月，第二轮战略对话在阿联酋首都阿布扎比举行。2014年1月，第三轮战略对话在北京举行，习近平主席会见了海合会代表团。双方一致同意致力于建立中国和海合会战略伙伴关系，强调要重启中国和海合会自贸区谈判进程，通过并签署了《中华人民共和国和海湾阿拉伯国家合作委员会成员国战略对话2014年至2017年行动计划》。海合会6个成员国是古丝绸之路的交汇地，地理位置重要，发展潜力巨大，是中国推进“一带一路”建设的天然和重要的合作伙伴。中国—海合会战略对话为双方共建“一带一路”提供了重要平台。

China-Gulf Cooperation Council Strategic Dialogue

The first round of China-Gulf Cooperation Council (GCC) Strategic Dialogue was held in Beijing in June 2010. The then Chinese Foreign Minister Yang Jiechi co-chaired the dialogue with the then Kuwaiti Deputy Prime Minister and Minister of Foreign Affairs Sheikh Mohammad Sabah Al-Salem Al-Sabah, Minister of State for Foreign Affairs of the United Arab Emirates Anwar Mohammed Qarqash, and the then GCC Secretary-General Abdul-Rahman al-Attiyah. They also signed a Memorandum of Understanding on Strategic Dialogue.

The second round of strategic dialogue was held in Abu Dhabi in May 2011, and the third round in Beijing in January 2014. President Xi Jinping met with the GCC delegation to the meeting. The two sides agreed to build a China-GCC strategic partnership and resume talks on a China-GCC free trade area. They also developed an action plan for cooperation from 2014 to 2017.

The six GCC member states are located where the ancient Silk Road routes converged. Their strategic location and their development potential make them natural and important partners for the Belt and Road Initiative. The China-GCC dialogue platform is therefore ideally suited for cooperation in this regard.

大湄公河次区域经济合作

大湄公河次区域经济合作是由澜沧江—湄公河流域内的6个国家，即中国、缅甸、老挝、泰国、柬埔寨、越南共同参与的一个次区域经济合作机制，成立于1992年。其宗旨是加强次区域国家的经济联系，促进次区域的经济和社会共同发展。亚洲开发银行是该机制的发起者、协调方和主要筹资方。领导人会议为最高决策机构，每3年召开1次，各成员国按照字母顺序轮流主办。日常决策机构为部长级会议，下设高官会、工作组和专题论坛等。该机制成立20多年来，在交通、能源、电力、基础设施、农业、旅游、信息通信、环境、人力资源开发、经济走廊等重点领

Greater Mekong Subregion Economic Cooperation

The Greater Mekong Subregion (GMS) Economic Cooperation is a subregional economic cooperation mechanism involving the six countries located at least partly within the river basin – China, Myanmar, Laos, Thailand, Cambodia and Vietnam. Established in 1992, it is designed to strengthen subregional economic ties and promote economic and social development in the subregion.

The program has been sponsored, coordinated and funded mainly by the Asian Development Bank. Its highest decision-making organ is the GMS Summit of Leaders, held every three years and hosted by a member state on the basis of alphabetical rotation. Policy direction for the program is discussed at the Ministerial Conference, under which meetings of senior officials and a range of working groups and forums in priority sectors are convened.

Since 1992, substantial progress has been achieved in implementing GMS projects in key areas such as transport, energy, power, infrastructure, agriculture, tourism, information and communications, environment, human resources development, and economic corridor development.

域开展了富有成效的合作。中国重视大湄公河次区域经济合作，积极参与各层次、各领域项目的规划与实施，为促进各成员国民生和福祉做出了自身的贡献。

China attaches great importance to the GMS economic cooperation, and actively participates in the planning and implementation of projects at different levels and in various fields, in an effort to improve the well-being of all member states.

中亚区域经济合作

中亚区域经济合作于1996年由亚洲开发银行发起成立，2002年提升为部长级合作，已建立起以部长会议、高官会议、行业协调委员会和区域工商圆桌会议为主的合作协调机制，是中亚区域重要的经济合作机制之一。其宗旨是以合作谋发展，通过促进交通运输、贸易、能源和其他重要领域的区域合作，促进成员国经济社会发展，减少贫困。现有成员包括中国、阿富汗、阿塞拜疆、巴基斯坦、蒙古国、哈萨克斯坦、吉尔吉斯斯坦、塔吉克斯坦、土库曼斯坦、乌兹别克斯坦和2016年加入的格鲁吉亚。世界银行、国际货币基金组织、联合国开发计划署、亚洲开发银行、欧洲复兴开发银行、伊斯兰开发银行6个国际组织，以及一些发达国家的双边援助机构作为发展伙伴也参与了该框架下的合作。

Central Asia Regional Economic Cooperation

The Central Asia Regional Economic Cooperation (CAREC) program was established in 1996 by the Asian Development Bank and upgraded to ministerial level in 2002. It has grown into a major mechanism for economic cooperation in Central Asia, with an institutional framework of the Ministerial Conference, the Senior Officials Meeting, coordinating committees in priority areas, and regional business roundtables.

CAREC envisions accelerated growth and poverty reduction through cooperation among member countries in transport, trade, energy and other key sectors.

CAREC countries include Afghanistan, Azerbaijan, China, Georgia, Kazakhstan, Kyrgyzstan, Mongolia, Pakistan, Tajikistan, Turkmenistan and Uzbekistan.

The World Bank, International Monetary Fund, United Nations Development Program, Asian Development Bank, European Bank for Reconstruction and Development, Islamic Development Bank, and some bilateral assistance organizations in developed countries have supported projects as partners under the CAREC program.

中国—中东欧国家合作

中国—中东欧国家合作简称“16+1合作”，是中国与中东欧16国之间建立的合作机制。在该机制框架下，17国将相互尊重各自主权独立和领土完整，加深对各自发展道路的理解，结合自身特点、需求和优先方向，本着平等协商、优势互补、合作共赢的原则，积极落实框架目标。“16+1合作”这一创新性的次区域合作机制，开辟了中国同传统友好国家关系发展的新途径，创新了中国同欧洲关系的实践，搭建了具有南北合作特点的南南合作新平台。近年来，在双方的共同努力下，“16+1合作”机制不断发展壮大，形成了全方位、宽领域、多层次的格局，已步入成熟期和早期收获期。实现“一带一路”倡议与

Cooperation Between China and Central and Eastern European Countries

The mechanism for cooperation between China and the Central and Eastern European (CEE) countries, commonly known as "16+1," has been established to facilitate collaboration between China and the 16 CEE countries on issues of common concern. The 17 countries agree to respect each other's sovereignty, independence, and territorial integrity, broaden understanding of each other's approach to development, and work to realize goals under the "16+1" framework in line with their own specific needs and priorities and based on equality, consultation, mutual complementarity, and cooperation for mutual benefit.

An innovative framework for subregional cooperation, the "16+1" opens new avenues for increased engagement between traditionally friendly countries. It is a platform that while focusing on South-South cooperation, also embraces South-North cooperation.

Thanks to the joint endeavors of the participants, the "16+1" has grown into an omni-dimensional, wide-ranging, and multi-channel framework that is harvesting fruitful results. A more effective alignment between

“16+1合作”机制的有效对接，将为中国—中东欧合作列车装载“超级引擎”，拓宽沿线国家的企业投资之路、贸易之路，开拓中国与中东欧国家的合作共赢之路。

the China-proposed Belt and Road Initiative and the “16+1” framework will create a super engine for the train of China-CEE cooperation, expand the channels of investment and trade for the countries along the route, and bring benefits to both China and the CEE countries.

中非合作论坛

为进一步加强中国与非洲国家的友好合作，共同应对经济全球化挑战，谋求共同发展，在中非双方共同倡议下，“中非合作论坛——北京2000年部长级会议”于2000年10月在北京召开，标志着中非合作论坛正式成立。该论坛的宗旨是平等互利、平等磋商、增进了解、扩大共识、加强友谊、促进合作。成员包括中国、与中国建交的53个非洲国家以及非洲联盟委员会。中非合作论坛部长级会议每三年举行一届，目前已举办七届。2015年12月4日，在中非合作论坛约翰内斯堡峰会开幕式上，习近平主席代表中国政府宣布，将中非新型战略伙伴关系提升为全面战略合作伙伴关系，提出与非洲在工业化、农业现代化、基础设施、金融、绿色发展、贸易和投资便利化、减贫惠民、公共卫生、人文、和平和安全等领域共同实施“十大合作计划”，规划了中非务实合作的新蓝

Forum on China-Africa Cooperation

The Forum on China-Africa Cooperation (FOCAC) was formally inaugurated at its first Ministerial Conference in October 2000 in Beijing, upon the joint initiative of China and Africa. It aims to further strengthen friendly cooperation between China and African countries to meet the challenges of economic globalization in search of common prosperity.

FOCAC promotes understanding, consensus-building, friendship and collaboration through consultation on the basis of equality.

FOCAC members include China, the 53 African states that have established diplomatic relations with China, and the Commission of the African Union. The FOCAC Ministerial Conference is held every three years, and to date seven conferences have been convened.

At the opening of the FOCAC Summit in Johannesburg (South Africa) on December 4, 2015, President Xi Jinping announced that the China-Africa new-type strategic partnership would be upgraded to a comprehensive strategic cooperative partnership. He also proposed 10 plans to boost cooperation with Africa in the areas of industrialization, agricultural modernization, infrastructure, financial services, green development, trade and investment facilitation, poverty reduction

图。2018年9月举行的第七届中非合作论坛北京峰会以“合作共赢，携手构建更加紧密的中非命运共同体”为主题。中国国家主席习近平出席开幕式并发表题为《携手共命运 同心促发展》的主旨讲话，强调中非要携起手来，共同打造责任共担、合作共赢、幸福共享、文化共兴、安全共筑、和谐共生的中非命运共同体，重点实施好产业促进、设施联通、贸易便利、绿色发展、能力建设、健康卫生、人文交流、和平安全“八大行动”。会议通过《关于构建更加紧密的中非命运共同体的北京宣言》和《中非合作论坛—北京行动计划（2019–2021年）》。

and public welfare, public health, people-to-people exchanges, and peace and security.

The Seventh FOCAC Summit was held in September 2018 in Beijing, on the theme of "China and Africa: Toward an Even Stronger Community with a Shared Future Through Win-Win Cooperation." Xi Jinping delivered a keynote speech entitled "Work Together for Common Development and Shared Future" at the opening session. He called for all parties to assume joint responsibility to build a China-Africa community of shared future that pursues win-win cooperation, delivers happiness for all, enjoys cultural prosperity and common security, and promotes harmony between man and nature.

To this end, China will launch eight initiatives in close collaboration with African countries: industrial promotion, infrastructure connectivity, trade facilitation, green development, capacity building, health care, people-to-people exchanges, and peace and security.

The summit adopted the Beijing Declaration – Toward an Even Stronger China-Africa Community with a Shared Future, and the Forum on China-Africa Cooperation Beijing Action Plan (2019-2021).

其他国家或组织倡议

Similar Initiatives

联合国“丝绸之路复兴计划”

复兴丝绸之路的计划早在20世纪60年代就已经开始，最初的计划是修建一条连接新加坡至土耳其的全长约14000千米的铁路。推动丝绸之路复兴的政府和组织数量众多，发挥作用最大的是联合国。2008年2月，联合国开发计划署正式发起了“丝绸之路复兴计划”，来自包括中国、俄罗斯、伊朗、土耳其在内的19国官员在瑞士日内瓦签署意向书，决定在今后数年投入430亿美元，激活古丝绸之路和其他一些古老的欧亚大陆通道，全长7000多千米。该计划由230个项目组成，期限为2008年至2014年，投资主要用于改善古丝绸之路等欧亚大陆通道的基础设施并开发多条经济走廊。该计划旨在使古老的丝绸之路重现辉煌，为中亚、东欧等国提供机会，并让欧亚大陆腹地分享全球化带来的好处。

United Nations: Silk Road Initiative

The Silk Road Initiative (SRI) was first discussed in the 1960s. The initial plan was to build 14,000 kilometers of railway line linking Singapore and Turkey. Many governments and organizations supported the initiative, with the United Nations playing the driving role.

The United Nations Development Program formally launched the SRI in February 2008. Officials from 19 countries including China, Russia, Iran and Turkey signed letters of intent in Geneva, Switzerland, committing to invest US$43 billion in the ensuing years to reinvigorate the ancient Silk Road and other Eurasian land arteries over a combined distance of more than 7,000 kilometers.

A total of 230 projects were planned from 2008 to 2014 to improve the infrastructure along the ancient trade routes and open a number of economic corridors. The ultimate goal was to bring a renaissance to the ancient routes, providing new development opportunities for Central Asian and East European countries, and enabling the inland areas to benefit from globalization.

俄罗斯"欧亚联盟"

2011年10月5日，时任俄罗斯总理普京在俄《消息报》发表署名文章，提出了"欧亚联盟"的发展理念。"欧亚联盟"旨在逐步融合独联体国家，打造统一的关税联盟和经济空间；通过提升独联体地区一体化的程度与层次，最终建立起拥有超国家机构的主权国家联盟。俄罗斯将以独联体国家为突破口，逐渐将"欧亚联盟"的范围由现在的俄罗斯、白俄罗斯、哈萨克斯坦、亚美尼亚、吉尔吉斯斯坦共5个前苏联加盟共和国扩大到整个前苏联"版图"，最后辐射到亚太地区。欧亚经济联盟作为"欧亚联盟"的关键环节，已于2015年正式启动，预计在2025年实现商品、服务、资金和劳动力的自由流动，最终将建成类似于欧盟的经济联盟，形成一个拥有1.7亿人口的统一市场。"欧亚联盟"与"一带一路"的战略对接前景广阔。丝绸之路经济带对于推动俄罗斯将经济发展的重心东移到西伯利亚和远东地区，缩小其亚洲部分与欧洲部分的经济差距，建成"欧亚联盟"有着重要意义。

Russia: Eurasian Union

The idea of a Eurasian Union was first proposed by the then Russian Prime Minister Vladimir Putin in an *Izvestia* op-ed, on October 5, 2011. It aims to integrate the member countries of the Commonwealth of Independent States (CIS) into a customs and economic union and ultimately to build a supra-national alliance of sovereign countries.

Russia's plan is to start with five CIS countries (Russia, Belarus, Kazakhstan, Armenia, and Kyrgyzstan), and then expand the Eurasian Union to include all former Soviet republics, and beyond that, to cover the Asia-Pacific region.

A central component of the Eurasian Union, the Eurasian Economic Union was launched in 2015. Free flow of products, services, capital and labor within the union is envisaged by 2025, and the final goal is to broaden the union into one similar to the European Union, with a unified market benefiting 170 million people.

The prospects for aligning the Eurasian Union framework with the Belt and Road Initiative appear promising. The latter will buttress Russia's efforts to shift the center of gravity of its economic development to Siberia and the Far East, to bridge the gap between its Asian and European parts, and to propel the process of building a fledgling Eurasian Union.

哈萨克斯坦“光明之路”

哈萨克斯坦总统纳扎尔巴耶夫在2014年11月发表的国情咨文中宣布，实行“光明之路”新经济政策，以大规模的投资计划促进哈萨克斯坦的经济增长。“光明之路”计划在3年之内将90亿美元分配到运输物流业建设、工业和能源基础设施建设、公共设施和水热供应网络改善、住房和社会基础设施建设、中小型企业扶持等方面。“光明之路”的核心在于对运输和物流基础设施项目的大规模投资，目的在于发展哈萨克斯坦的国内运输网络，并将哈萨克斯坦打造成连接中国、欧洲与中东各大市场的全球交通走廊。哈萨克斯坦决策者预计“光明之路”的实施将使沿中国、中亚、俄罗斯和欧洲线路运输的货运量翻一番，达到每年3300万吨。中哈两国领导人多次指出，“光明之路”与“一带一路”有众多契合点和互补性。双方表达了对接的强烈意愿，并已采取务实措施。

Kazakhstan: "Bright Road" Initiative

In November 2014, President Nazarbayev of Kazakhstan announced an economic policy called "Bright Road," intended to spur the country's economic growth by means of large-scale investment.

The "Bright Road" Initiative plans to spend US$9 billion over a period of three years on transport, logistics, industrial and energy infrastructure, public facilities, water and heating supply, housing, public services, and small and medium enterprises. The huge investment will upgrade Kazakhstan's transport network and make the country a global transit corridor connecting markets in China, Europe and the Middle East.

Kazakhstan's decision-makers expect that the initiative will double the freight transported through the country to China, Central Asia, Russia and Europe, to 33 million tons per year. They and their Chinese counterparts agree that the "Bright Road" Initiative and the Belt and Road Initiative are complementary and mutually reinforcing. They have expressed a strong desire to seek a better alignment of the two, and practical measures are being taken in this regard.

蒙古国"草原之路"

2014年11月，蒙古国提出基于地处欧亚之间的地理优势，准备实施"草原之路"计划，旨在通过运输和贸易振兴蒙古国经济。"草原之路"计划由5个项目组成，总投资需求约为500亿美元，具体包括：建设长达997千米的高速公路直通中俄，新建输电线路1100千米，在蒙古现有铁路基础上进行扩展，对天然气和石油管道进行扩建。蒙古国政府认为，"草原之路"计划将为蒙古国新建交通干道沿线地区带来更多的商机，并可带动当地各类产业的升级改造。蒙古国的核心产业即能源和矿业也会享受到此计划带来的直接好处，甚至使这些产业得到新的腾飞。中蒙两国领导人多次表示，"一带一路"与"草原之路"高度契合，符合双方共同发展利益。

Mongolia: "Steppe Road" Program

Unveiled in November 2014, Mongolia's "Steppe Road" Program relies on the country's strategically important location on the Eurasian continent to reinvigorate its economy by improving transport and trade.

With an estimated investment of US$50 billion, projects envisioned under the "Steppe Road" Program include a 997-kilometer-long expressway linking China and Russia, 1,100 kilometers of power transmission lines, and expansion of existing railways as well as gas and oil pipelines.

The Mongolian government believes that the program will bring business opportunities to the areas the new arteries traverse, and improve productivity in many sectors. It will benefit, in particular, Mongolia's pillar industries – energy and mining – and provide them with a launching pad for transformational change. As the leaders of China and Mongolia have affirmed on multiple occasions, the Belt and Road Initiative and the "Steppe Road" Program dovetail neatly with each other and will contribute to the development of both countries.

印度"季风计划"

"季风计划"是印度莫迪政府尝试"借古谋今"的一种外交战略新构想，设想在从南亚次大陆到整个环印度洋的广大区域内，打造以印度为主导的环印度洋地区互利合作新平台。"季风计划"以深受印度文化影响的环印度洋地区及该地区国家间悠久的贸易往来历史为依托，以印度为主力，推进环印度洋地区国家间在共同开发海洋资源、促进经贸往来等领域的合作。莫迪政府的"季风计划"已从最初的文化项目定位发展成为具有外交、经济功能的准战略规划。印度是古代"海上丝路"的重要驿站，也是中国共建共享"一带一路"的重要伙伴。"季风计划"与"一带一路"在结构和本质上并不具有天然的对抗性，反而能实现相互对接甚至融合。

India: Project Mausam

Project Mausam is a foreign policy initiative of the Indian government under Narendra Modi. It envisions a new platform for cooperation in the vast area extending from the South Asian subcontinent to other parts of the Indian Ocean littoral, in which India will play the leading role.

Rooted in the history of trade among the littoral countries deeply influenced by Indian culture, the project pushes for renewed collaboration among these countries in the exploration of maritime resources, and trade. Initially proposed as a cultural program, Project Mausam is now evolving into a quasi-strategic initiative with diplomatic and economic reverberations.

India was a major staging post on the ancient Silk Road routes on the sea, and today it is an important partner of China in advancing the Belt and Road Initiative. There is no conflict between "Project Mausam" and China's initiative in either structure or nature; on the contrary the two can be readily aligned and even integrated.

俄印伊“北南走廊计划”

“北南走廊计划”最早由俄罗斯、印度、伊朗三国于2000年发起，计划修建一条从南亚途经中亚、高加索、俄罗斯到达欧洲的货运通道。“北南走廊”规划全长5000多千米，预计建成后较现在的欧亚运输路线缩短40%，其运费也将相应减少30%。该运输走廊将北起芬兰湾的圣彼得堡，经俄南部的里海港口阿斯特拉罕，跨里海至伊朗北部的诺乌舍赫尔港，再南下至伊朗南部港口城市阿巴斯，穿过阿曼湾，最后经阿拉伯海抵达印度港口孟买，其中包括公路、铁路、海运等多种运输形式。该运输走廊计划将印度西海岸港口和伊朗在阿拉伯海的阿巴斯港和查赫巴尔港连接起来。该计划自提出以来就因资金迟滞、政治分歧，尤其是处在核心位置的伊朗态度日渐消极而一直进展缓慢，以至于在相当长时间里，各方都没有就实际运作方案达成共识。2011年，印度的积极推动使该计划重获生机。近年来，已经有包括中亚国家在内的16个国家参与到这个项目中。但是，印度积极推动的“北南走廊计

Russia-India-Iran: North-South Corridor

Initiated by Russia, India and Iran in 2000, the North-South Corridor is intended to be a freight and cargo transit route, stretching from South Asia to Central Asia, the Caucasus and Russia, and ending in Europe.

The proposed route has an estimated length of over 5,000 kilometers, 40 percent shorter than the length of the current Eurasian transit, and is expected to cut transport costs by 30 percent. It stretches southward from St. Petersburg by the Gulf of Finland to cross the Caspian Sea from the southern Russian port of Astrakhan to northern Iran's Now Shahr port, onward to the Port of Bandar Abbas in south Iran, then across the Gulf of Oman and the Arabian Sea to reach the port of Mumbai in India. It will also connect India's western coast ports and Iran's ports of Bandar Abbas and Chabahar on the Arabian Sea. A multi-modal transport system is envisioned integrating motorway and rail transport and ocean shipping services.

The project has, however, experienced delays due to lack of capital and political differences. As Iran is centrally located, its lukewarm response, in particular, contributed to a protracted failure to reach consensus on any specific action plan.

The project gained traction again in 2011 on the back of India's renewed push. Sixteen

划”因与巴基斯坦存有潜在冲突，发展前景不被看好。

countries including those in Central Asia have now joined. But the prospects are dimmed by the potential conflicts between India and Pakistan.

欧盟“南部能源走廊”

“南部能源走廊”也称“南部走廊输气网”，是欧盟一直倡导的大型重点项目，旨在减少对单一国家的天然气依赖，实现欧洲能源供应渠道的多元化。欧盟在与相关国家谈判多年后，于2008年提出建设一个以纳布科天然气管道为主的“南部走廊”输气管道网络。纳布科天然气管道项目由欧盟投资，全长约3300千米，目的是将里海地区的天然气经土耳其、保加利亚、罗马尼亚和匈牙利输送至奥地利后，再输往欧盟其他国家。该项目预计投资总额为79亿欧元，年输送天然气能力为310亿立方米。当前，在气源选择、管道过境以及国际环境等方面，欧盟“南部能源走廊”构想依旧存在诸多掣肘，供气计划障碍重重，欧盟实现能源安全之路任重道远。

European Union: Southern Gas Corridor

The Southern Gas Corridor is a major initiative by the European Union (EU) to diversify its energy supply, and thereby reduce its dependence on a single supplier.

After years of talks between the EU and countries concerned, a plan was proposed in 2008 to build a southern corridor, with projects including the Nabucco Gas Pipeline. This EU-funded 3,300-kilometer-long pipeline project seeks to ship gas from the Caspian Sea to Austria and onward to other European countries via Turkey, Bulgaria, Romania and Hungary. With an estimated investment of 7.9 billion euros, the pipeline is expected to deliver 31 billion cubic meters of natural gas annually.

There are still daunting challenges in selecting sources of supply and pipeline routes and addressing international dynamics before the concept of this corridor can become a reality. The EU's path to energy security remains protracted.

美国“新丝绸之路计划”

美国“新丝绸之路计划”起源于霍普金斯大学弗雷德里克•斯塔尔教授于2005年提出的“新丝绸之路”构想。2011年7月，时任美国国务卿希拉里在印度参加第二次美印战略对话期间正式提出了“新丝绸之路计划”：以阿富汗为中心，通过中亚和南亚在政治、安全、能源、交通等领域的合作，建立一个由亲美的、实行市场经济和世俗政治体制的国家组成的新地缘政治板块，推动包括阿富汗在内的中亚地区国家的经济社会发展，以服务于美国在该地区的战略利益。同年10月，美国国务院向美国驻有关国家大使馆发出电报，要求将美国的中亚、南亚政策统一命名为“新丝绸之路”战略，并将其向国际伙伴通报。这标志着“新丝绸之路计划”正式成为美国的官方政策。目前，“新丝绸之路计划”的部分项目已经完工，如乌兹别克斯坦—阿富汗铁路已经竣工，塔吉克斯坦桑土达水电站已开始向阿富汗送电。从美国的官方表态及实际进展来看，该计划虽然面临许多困难和风险，如地区内国家基础设施落后、资金不足、相互缺乏信任，以及恐怖

United States: New Silk Road Initiative

The US New Silk Road Initiative was originally conceived by Frederick Starr, a Johns Hopkins University scholar, in 2005.

The initiative was formally announced by the then US Secretary of State Hillary Clinton in July 2011 at the Second US-India Strategic Dialogue in India. It aims to build a new geopolitical block consisting of the pro-US market economies with secular political systems. With a special focus on Afghanistan, it seeks to expand cooperation among Central and South Asian countries in areas such as energy and transport as well as on political and security issues to boost local economic and social development and serve US strategic interests in the region.

In October of the same year, the US Department of State instructed US embassies in the countries concerned to rebrand its Central and South Asia policies under the New Silk Road framework, and to notify international partners accordingly. Such a move marked the formal inclusion of the New Silk Road Initiative in US official policies.

Some of the New Silk Road Initiative projects have now been completed, including the Uzbekistan-Afghanistan Railway and Tajikistan's Sangtuda Hydropower Station, which is already supplying power to Afghanistan. Judging by official releases

主义和极端主义肆虐等，但美国从未明确放弃该计划。

and the progress of the initiative, the US has shown no intention of giving it up despite challenges in terms of backward support infrastructure, insufficient funds, lack of mutual trust, and terrorist and extremist threats in the region.

韩国"丝绸之路快速铁路"

时任韩国总统朴槿惠于2013年10月提出了名为"丝绸之路快速铁路"的构想，旨在构建连接韩国、朝鲜、俄罗斯、中国、中亚、欧洲的丝绸之路快速铁路，并在欧亚地区构建电力、天然气和输油管线等能源网络。"丝绸之路快速铁路"是韩国"欧亚倡议"的核心内容之一，它以铁路为中心，通过铁路、道路、港口及航空构筑起一体化的物流运输交通体系。韩国的"丝绸之路快速铁路"计划因朝韩关系停滞、"欧亚倡议"落地困难等原因而踟蹰不前。作为中国的近邻，韩国政府和企业对"一带一路"建设的关注正在逐步增加。

South Korea: "Silk Road Express"

In October 2013, the then South Korean President Park Geun-hye proposed building a "Silk Road Express" to connect railways in South Korea, North Korea, Russia, China, Central Asia and Europe, and create an energy network of power grids and gas and oil pipelines in Eurasia. This is a core element of South Korea's "Eurasia Initiative," which intends to integrate rail, roads, ports and aviation into a unified system of logistics solutions.

The "Silk Road Express" project has, however, been put on the back burner due to the troubled relationship between the two neighbors on the Korean peninsula, and the difficulties in implementing the Eurasia Initiative. Meanwhile, the government and businesses of South Korea, a close neighbor of China, are showing growing interest in China's Belt and Road Initiative.

日本“丝绸之路外交”

日本“丝绸之路外交”由时任首相桥本龙太郎于1997年首次提出，初衷是保障日本能源来源的多元化。桥本龙太郎倡议把中亚及高加索八国称为“丝绸之路地区”，并将其置于日本新外交战略的重要位置。此后，日本对中亚的外交逐渐被称为“丝绸之路外交”。日本提出这一战略有如下意图：一是从经济利益考虑出发，保障自身能源来源的多元化，抢先占据中亚地区这个储量不亚于中东的能源宝库；二是从地缘政治着眼，谋求日本在中亚和高加索地区站稳脚跟。2004年，日本重提“丝绸之路外交”战略，并推动设立“中亚+日本”合作机制，旨在通过加强政治影响和经济渗透来争取中亚地区的能源开发与贸易主导权。2012年，日本向“丝绸之路地区”提供2191.3万美元的政府发展援助，投资领域涉及道路、机场、桥梁、发电站、

Japan: Silk Road Diplomacy

The concept of Japan's Silk Road Diplomacy was first introduced in 1997 by Hashimoto Ryutaro, the then Japanese Prime Minister, to ensure Japan's access to diverse sources of energy supply. The plan covers the eight countries in Central Asia and the Caucasus, referred to as the "Silk Road region," and places them high on Japan's new foreign policy agenda. This Silk Road Diplomacy has since defined Japan's diplomatic engagement with Central Asia.

The objective of this strategy is twofold: to ensure diverse sources of energy supply by securing access to the treasure house of Central Asia (which has larger reserves of oil than the Middle East) so as to protect Japan's economic interests; and to establish a strong geopolitical presence in Central Asia and the Caucasus.

In 2004, Japan's Silk Road Diplomacy gained new momentum with the launch of the "Central Asia Plus Japan" dialogue in an effort to increase Japan's political influence and economic penetration and gain a leading role in energy development and trade in Central Asia. In 2012, Japan provided US$21.91 million worth of government development assistance to build roads, airports, bridges, power plants and canals in the Silk Road region. In October 2015, Prime Minister Abe

运河等基础设施建设。2015年10月，安倍晋三出访蒙古和中亚五国，目的是要激活“日本与中亚对话”机制，促进运输和物流等领域合作，这表明“日本针对中国的‘跟跑外交’策略已在中亚拉开帷幕”。

Shinzo visited Mongolia and five Central Asian countries with the mission of reinvigorating the "Central Asia Plus Japan" dialogue focusing on cooperation in transport and logistics. These moves have been interpreted as Japan's attempt to counter China's Central Asia policy.

合作案例

Projects Under Way

中白工业园

2010年3月，时任中国国家副主席习近平到访白俄罗斯，白俄罗斯政府希望能够借鉴中国—新加坡苏州工业园区的模式，在其境内建立中白工业园。2011年9月18日，两国政府签订了关于中白工业园的协定。2012年8月27日，中白工业园区开发股份有限公司成立。2014年6月19日，该工业园在明斯克奠基。2015年5月10日，习近平主席在与卢卡申科总统会谈时，建议推动两国发展战略对接，共建丝绸之路经济带，把中白工业园建设作为合作重点，发挥政府间协调机制作用，谋划好园区未来发展，将园区项目打造成丝绸之路经济带上的明珠和双方互利合作的典范。中白工业园是中国在海外建设的层次最高、开发面积最大、政策条件最为优越的工业园区。该工业园总面积91.5平方千米，国际公路、洲际公路、铁路穿越园区，连接欧亚经济联盟与欧盟国家，具有良好的区位优势，是迄今为止中国在海外投资建设规模

China-Belarus Industrial Park

During the then Vice President Xi Jinping's visit to Belarus in March 2010, the Belarusian government expressed interest in opening an industrial park in Belarus modeled on the China-Singapore Industrial Park in Suzhou, Jiangsu Province. An agreement was signed by both governments on September 18, 2011, and a joint venture, China-Belarus Industrial Park Development Company, was established on August 27, 2012. A ground-breaking ceremony was held in Minsk on June 19, 2014.

During talks with Belarusian President Lukashenko on May 10, 2015, Xi Jinping, who had become President by then, proposed enhancing the strategic alignment between China and Belarus in a joint effort to build the Silk Road Economic Belt, with the construction of the industrial park as a focus area. He went on to emphasize the importance of coordination between both governments in planning the park so as to showcase the advantages of cooperation.

Occupying an area of 91.5 square kilometers, it is the largest industrial park in which China has invested overseas, with the highest concentration of high-tech businesses. It also enjoys favorable policy incentives. Strategically situated, it connects the Eurasian Economic Union countries and

最大的产业园区。中白工业园将以先进制造业和现代服务业为支撑，吸引和积聚智力资源，建成集“生态、宜居、兴业、活力、创新”五位一体的国际新城。目前，中白工业园已有34家企业入园，到2020年将实现100家的目标。

the European Union members, offering easy access to international and transcontinental highways and railways.

Focused on advanced manufacturing and services, and attracting international talent and resources, the park is intended to be a new international city, an environmentally friendly, vibrant community that embraces entrepreneurship and innovation, and an ideal place to live.

To date, 34 enterprises have moved into the park, and the number will reach 100 by 2020.

瓜达尔港自由区

2013年5月，在李克强总理出访巴基斯坦过程中，双方同意共同建设“中巴经济走廊”，开展能源、交通基建等多个方面的合作。2015年4月，习近平主席出访巴基斯坦，进一步推进两国合作事宜。作为“中巴经济走廊”重点项目之一和瓜达尔港开发项目的重要组成部分，瓜达尔港自由区将以港口为依托，重点发展商贸物流、加工贸易、仓储和金融等产业。根据建设规划，瓜达尔港自由区总占地面积约为923公顷，分四期进行建设。一期项目（起步区）已于2018年1月举行开园仪式。中国海外港口控股有限公司投入近2.5亿美元，在短短1年之内完成了面积25英亩，集合路、水、电、通讯、安全围网、垃圾处理等功能的现代园区建设。目前，酒店、银行、保险公司、金融租赁、物流、海外仓、粮油加工、渔业加工、家电组装等30多家中、巴企业已入驻园区，直接投资额超过30亿人民币。入驻企业全部投产后，年产值将超

Gwadar Port Free Zone

During Premier Li Keqiang's visit to Pakistan in May 2013, China and Pakistan agreed to build the China-Pakistan Economic Corridor to promote energy and transportation infrastructure development, among other projects. During President Xi Jinping's visit in April 2015, closer bilateral cooperation was again highlighted. A key element of the China-Pakistan Economic Corridor and an essential component of the Gwadar Port development project, the free zone aims to improve trade logistics, facilitate processing trade, and promote warehousing and financial services.

According to the project plan, the free zone will occupy an area of 923 hectares and be developed in four phases. The first phase opened for operation in January 2018. The China Overseas Ports Holding Ltd. had invested nearly US$250 million and built a 25-acre modern industrial park complete with roads, water pipes, electricity, communications, security fence and waste disposal facilities. More than 30 Chinese and Pakistani enterprises have moved in, with 3 billion yuan of direct investment. These include hotel, bank, insurance, financial leasing, logistics, overseas warehousing, grain and oil processing, aquatic product processing, and home appliances assembly. Their yearly output value will exceed 5 billion yuan once they all come into operation.

过50亿人民币。瓜达尔港自由区将采用类似深圳蛇口的建设模式，形成一个包括“港口+园区+城区”的综合体。建成后的瓜达尔港自由区将带动俾路支省乃至巴基斯坦全国的整体发展。

The free zone will be modeled after the Shekou Industrial Zone in Shenzhen, China, comprising a port, an industrial park, and residential and business areas. Once completed, it will spur economic growth in Balochistan and the rest of Pakistan.

科伦坡港口城

科伦坡港口城由中国交通建设集团和斯里兰卡政府联合开发，是斯里兰卡目前最大的外国投资项目，位于首都科伦坡核心商贸区，占地面积269公顷，通过在科伦坡港口附近填海造地的方式，规划金融区、中央公园区、宜居生活岛、游艇码头区、国际品牌带动区等五大主题区域；建造布局设计精湛的甲级写字楼、医疗中心、教育机构、休闲娱乐综合体、游艇码头、购物胜地、豪华酒店等世界级的城市设施和配套项目，总建筑面积预计将达到565万平方米。科伦坡港口城一期填海造地投资约14亿美元，预计可带动二期开发投资达130亿美元。该项目由中国交通建设集团有限公司与斯里兰卡国家港务局共同开发。工程整体工期约25年，于2014年9月17日开工，后因斯里兰卡大选以及政府更迭等因素影响，建设进展有所延宕。经中方多方面交涉，在2016年8月签署新的三方协议后，该工程项目得以继续推进。项目复工后，中方为尽快完成填海造地工程，动用4艘超大型高科技耙吸挖泥船，不分昼夜工作。2018年1月，科伦坡港口城269公顷

Colombo Port City

Colombo Port City is a project implemented by the China Communications Construction Company Limited and the Sri Lanka Ports Authority. It is currently Sri Lanka's largest foreign investment project located in Colombo's central business district. It will be built on 269 hectares of land reclaimed from the sea adjacent to the existing Port of Colombo. The whole city will have five functional zones: a financial district, a central park, an island for residence, a marina and a zone of international brands. There will be a yacht marina, a shopping mall, a medical center, schools, office buildings, luxury hotels and amusement facilities.

The Port City will have a combined floor area of 5.65 million square meters, with an initial investment of US$1.4 billion. It is expected to attract US$13 billion of further development investment.

The entire construction will continue for 25 years. After ground-breaking on September 17, 2014, the project was delayed as a result of Sri Lanka's general election and subsequent transfer of power to a new administration. After repeated efforts by China, a new tripartite agreement to proceed with the construction of the project was signed in August 2016. When construction was resumed, the Chinese side employed four extra-large trailing suction hopper dredgers

吹填土地已全部形成，填海工程完工标志着整体项目工程取得重大进展。

that worked day and night. By January 2018, 269 hectares of land had been reclaimed from the sea, signifying major overall progress.

中欧班列

2011年3月，自重庆出发的首趟中欧班列从新疆阿拉山口口岸出境，标志着铁路开始成为海运、空运之外连接亚欧大陆的第三条运输大道。此后，在“一带一路”倡议的推动下，中欧班列进入高速发展期。2015年3月中国发布的《推动共建丝绸之路经济带和21世纪海上丝绸之路的愿景与行动》，明确将中欧班列建设列为国家发展重点。2016年6月8日起，中国铁路正式启用“中欧班列”统一品牌。截至2018年年底，中欧班列已有65条线路经新疆、内蒙古、东北三个方向出境，通往中亚、俄罗斯、中东欧、西欧等地，累计开行已突破1.3万列，运送货物80万标箱，国内开行城市59个，到达欧洲15个国家49个城市，运输网络覆盖亚欧大陆主要区域。中欧班列作为

China Railway Express to Europe

The launch of a rail freight service from the Chinese city Chongqing via the Alashankou border crossing in Xinjiang through Central Asia to Europe in March 2011 ushered in a new era for freight on rail as an alternative to shipping by sea or air. China-Europe rail cargo transport has subsequently gained rapid traction, fueled by the rollout of the Belt and Road Initiative.

The importance of China's rail link to Europe was highlighted in a white paper issued by the Chinese government in March 2015 entitled *Joining Hands to Build a Silk Road Economic Belt and a 21st Century Maritime Silk Road – Vision and Actions*. The name "China Railway Express" was formally introduced on June 8, 2016, for all Europe-bound trains.

By the end of 2018, 65 service lines were running through Xinjiang, Inner Mongolia and Northeast China border crossings to destinations in Central Asia, Russia, Central and Eastern Europe and Western Europe. More than 13,000 trains had made the trans-continental voyage between 59 Chinese cities and 49 cities in 15 European countries, transporting nearly 800,000 standard containers of goods. The network covers major regions on the Eurasian continent.

“铁轨上的‘一带一路’”，架起了中国与欧洲、世界联系的桥梁，推进了中国与沿线国家的互联互通。它不再只是一条条开放的线段，而是已形成一张开放的网络；它不仅发挥着货物运输通道的功能，而且将承担更多的使命：吸纳全球资金、资源、技术、人才等产业要素，发挥全球产业衔接功能。

The “China Railway Express” service, seen as the “Belt and Road on rail,” helps boost connectivity between China and Europe and the rest of the world. An interconnected network has begun to replace uncoordinated individual cargo lines. In addition to offering freight transport solutions, it contributes to flows of global investment, resources, technology and skilled personnel, and facilitates global cross-sector collaboration.

雅万高铁

雅万高铁连接印尼首都雅加达和旅游名城万隆，全长142千米，最高设计时速350千米，建成通车后，从雅加达至万隆的时间将缩短为约40分钟。雅万高铁是中国高铁方案走出去的“第一单”。它采用中国铁路技术标准，按照当地的气候、线路条件、沿线群众文化传统和生活习惯为印尼“量身打造”，建成后将成为印尼乃至东南亚的第一条高速铁路，对当地经济发展和社会进步产生巨大的推动作用。2015年10月16日，中国铁路总公司在雅加达与印度尼西亚4家国有企业签署协议，组建中国—印尼雅万高铁合资公司，负责印尼雅加达至万隆高速铁路项目的建设和运营。雅万高铁项目是国际上首个由政府主导搭台、两国企业间进行合作建设的高铁项目，是国际铁路合作模式的一次探索和创新。2016年1月21日，雅万高铁项目开工奠基。截至2019年1月，雅万高铁项目实施的工作机制已基本到位，项目许可、融资、征地拆迁等关键事项扎实推进，22处控制性工程取得突破，项目建设进入全面推进实施新阶段。雅万高铁不仅将直接拉动印尼

Jakarta-Bandung High-Speed Railway

The Jakarta-Bandung high-speed railway is a 142-kilometer rail line linking Indonesia's capital Jakarta to Bandung, a tourist destination. Thanks to a design speed of 350 kilometers per hour, once the project is completed the travel time between the two hubs will be cut to about 40 minutes.

This is the first overseas project to be built with Chinese high-speed rail technology, with design considerations given to local climate and conditions, and the traditions and habits of local residents. The first high-speed rail project in Indonesia and all of Southeast Asia, it is expected to greatly boost local economic and social development.

An agreement was reached on October 16, 2015 between China Railway Co. and four Indonesian state-owned enterprises to establish a Chinese-Indonesian consortium tasked to construct and operate the line. The project represents an innovative approach to international cooperation, with businesses from both countries involved under the sponsorship of the two governments.

A ground-breaking ceremony was held on January 21, 2016. By January 2019, a working mechanism was in place to boost the project, with progress in project permit, fund-raising, land requisition and demolition, and breakthroughs in 22 key projects.

冶炼、制造、基建、电力、物流等配套产业发展，增加就业机会，推动产业结构升级，而且在建成通车后，还将形成一个新的高铁经济走廊和涵盖周边、充满活力的双城经济体，极大地便利这一地区人们的出行，丰富他们的生活，带动沿线旅游产业快速发展，并为中国—印尼之间在基础设施、商贸等领域的进一步合作奠定良好基础。

The rail link is expected to stimulate growth in such sectors as metallurgy, manufacturing, infrastructure, power generation and logistics, create jobs, and promote structural transformation in Indonesia. It will, in particular, facilitate travel and promote tourism along the rail line, supporting a high-speed rail economic corridor and a twin-city cluster. It will also provide a sound basis for further cooperation between China and Indonesia in such fields as infrastructure development and trade.

中老铁路

中老铁路起于老中边境口岸磨丁，向南到达老挝首都万象，正线建筑长度414.332千米，其中62.7%以上路段为桥梁和隧道，设计时速160千米，全线采用中国管理标准和技术标准建设，总投资近400亿人民币，建设工期5年，2016年12月全线开工，2017年年中进入全面施工状态，计划在2021年12月建成通车。由中老两国合资的老中铁路有限公司负责全线建设和运营管理，由中老双方按70%和30%的股比合资建设。中老铁路不仅是第一个以中方为主投资建设、共同运营并与中国铁路网直接联通的境外铁路项目，也是继印尼雅万高铁项目之后第二个全面采用中国标准、中国技术和装备的国际铁路建设项目。该条线路同时也将成为泛亚铁路网的重要组成部分。中老铁路项目建成后，一方面将极大地带动老挝经济社会发展，提高当地运输效率和水平，扩大和提升中老两国在经济、贸易、投资、旅游等领域的合作，进一步增强中国—东盟自贸区的经济联系；

China-Laos Railway

Starting from the Mohan-Boten crossing at the China-Laos border, the 414-kilometer-long China-Laos railway will run south to Vientiane, capital of Laos. It is scheduled to open in December 2021, with a design speed of 160 kilometers per hour. The investment in the project will be about 40 billion yuan (US$5.76 billion), 70 percent of which comes from China and the remainder from Laos.

The construction officially got underway in December 2016, and over 62.7 percent of the railway will consist of bridges and tunnels. The Laos-China Railway Co. Ltd. is responsible for the construction and operation of the line.

This line is China's first overseas railway project to provide a direct link to China's internal rail network, and the second such project – after the Jakarta-Bandung high-speed rail link in Indonesia – to be built with Chinese standards, management, technology and equipment. It will also be an important section of the pan-Asia railway network.

Once in service, the railway will significantly boost the economic and social development of Laos, facilitate local transportation and improve its efficiency, and expand cooperation between China and Laos in areas such as trade, investment and tourism. It will contribute to the development

另一方面也将为中国西南地区经济发展注入新的动力。

of the China-ASEAN Free Trade Area, and inject new life into the economy in China's southwest region.

中泰铁路

中泰铁路是中国与泰国合作建设的泰国首条标准轨高速铁路，修建计划从曼谷至廊开约867千米。2012年，时任泰国总理英拉访华，两国提出“大米换高铁”计划，但随着泰国政局的动荡，这一计划被搁置。2014年12月6日，泰国国家立法议会批准中泰铁路合作谅解备忘录草案。同年12月19日，李克强总理和巴育总理共同见证了《中泰铁路合作谅解备忘录》的签署，随后，中泰铁路进入正式协商阶段。2015年12月19日，中泰铁路项目在泰国举行了启动仪式。2016年年初，中泰铁路曼谷—呵叻段开工建设，大约3年内完工，而整条线路将在5年内建设完成。中泰铁路合作项目是中国“一带一路”倡议与泰国巴育政府基础设施建设规划有效对接的范例。中泰铁路主要途经泰国东北部地区，所经站点均为泰国重要城市，因此将大大促进泰国东北部经济发展，惠及民生。

China-Thailand Railway

The China-Thailand railway will be Thailand's first standard-gauge railway to be jointly built by China and Thailand. Its planned length is about 867 kilometers.

A "rice for high-speed rail" plan was first proposed by both countries in 2012 during the visit of the then Thai Prime Minister Yingluck Shinawatra to China. The plan was then shelved as a result of political turmoil in Thailand. After approval by the Thai Parliament on December 6, 2014, a memorandum of understanding for the rail project was signed on December 19. The signing was witnessed by Chinese Premier Li Keqiang and Thai Prime Minister Prayut Chan-o-cha. Formal consultation on the project followed.

A ground-breaking ceremony was held in Thailand on December 19, 2015. The construction of the Bangkok-Kaeng Khoi section began in early 2016, and is scheduled to be completed in three years. The entire rail system is expected to be operational in five years.

This rail cooperation project will be a showcase for effective alignment between China's Belt and Road Initiative and Thailand's infrastructure development plans. Serving Thailand's northeastern regions and covering major cities, the network will be a great boon to economic development and standards of living in those regions.

蒙内铁路

蒙内铁路是东非铁路网的起始段，全长471千米，设计运力2500万吨，设计客运时速120千米、货运时速80千米，连接肯尼亚首都内罗毕和东非第一大港蒙巴萨港，是首条在海外全部采用“中国标准”建造的铁路。它因为是肯尼亚百年来修建的第一条新铁路，所以有该国“世纪铁路”之称。该铁路于2014年10月正式开工建设，2017年6月1日开通试运行。截至2018年11月，蒙内铁路自运营以来，开行旅客列车1762列，已经安全运行84.6万千米，较原规划提前10个月完成发送旅客200万人次的运输指标，这相当于内罗毕350万人口中每7人就有4人乘坐过蒙内铁路旅客列车。建成后，蒙巴萨到内罗毕从原先的10多个小时缩短到4个多小时，降低物流成本超过40%，而铁路的建设拉动了肯尼亚国内生产总值1.5%至2%的增长，更为关键的是，通过铁路形成了包括港口在内的全产业链

Mombasa-Nairobi Railway

The 471-kilometer-long Mombasa-Nairobi rail is the first section of a planned East Africa railway network. Passenger trains travel at 120 kilometers per hour, while freight trains run at 80 kilometers per hour and are able to carry 25 million tons per year. Connecting Nairobi, the capital city of Kenya, with Mombasa, the largest port in East Africa, it is the first rail line with Chinese standards ever built outside of China. It is also the first new rail line in Kenya in a century.

The project started in October 2014, and the railway opened to traffic on June 1, 2017. It cuts the travel time from Mombasa to Nairobi from over 10 hours to a little more than four hours. By November 2018, 1,762 trains had safely run 846,000 kilometers and transported 2 million passengers, meeting the target passenger number 10 months ahead of time. On average, four sevenths of Nairobi's 3.5 million residents have travelled by this line.

Construction of the Mombasa-Nairobi section has created nearly 30,000 jobs in Kenya and boosted annual GDP growth by 1.5-2 percent. The cost of movement of goods has been reduced by 40 percent since the completion of this initial project. More importantly, a whole industry chain including ports has taken shape with the construction

发展。根据远期规划，该铁路将连接肯尼亚、坦桑尼亚、乌干达、卢旺达、布隆迪和南苏丹等东非6国，促进东非现代化铁路网的形成和地区经济发展。据统计，蒙内铁路建设期间，为肯尼亚带来近3万个就业机会，年均拉动国内生产总值增长1.5%。

of the railway.

A long-term masterplan envisions a rail system serving six East African countries, namely Kenya, Tanzania, Uganda, Rwanda, Burundi and South Sudan. This modern network will help promote economic development in East Africa and beyond.

亚的斯—阿达玛高速公路

亚的斯—阿达玛高速公路是埃塞俄比亚乃至东非地区首条高速公路。这条高速公路由中国政府融资支持，全部采用中国技术和标准承建，按双向6车道、时速120千米标准建设，是埃塞俄比亚第一条现代化高速公路，也是东非地区规模最大、等级最高的高速公路。该条公路连通埃塞俄比亚首都亚的斯亚贝巴和该国第二大城市阿达玛，公路通车后，从亚的斯亚贝巴到阿达玛的时间由2.5小时缩短为45分钟，对改善埃塞俄比亚民众出行、提高运输效率及吸引外商投资发挥着重要作用。该公路全长100多千米，一期和二期项目分别于2014年5月和2016年8月竣工。项目实施中，承建的中国企业不仅雇用大量本地劳动力，也对埃塞俄比亚输出了技术和管理经验，有助于埃塞俄比亚加强基建能力建设。

Addis Ababa-Adama Expressway

The Addis Ababa-Adama expressway is the first expressway in Ethiopia, and it is of the highest grade in East Africa. The road was built with financing support from the Chinese government and using Chinese technology and standards.

Connecting Ethiopia's capital Addis Ababa to its second largest city Adama, the expressway has facilitated the travel of people, improved transportation efficiency, and enhanced Ethiopia's ability to attract foreign investment. With a design speed of 120 kilometers per hour, the six-lane expressway has shortened the travel time from 2.5 hours to 45 minutes. The two phases of the construction of the over-100-kilometer-long road were completed in May 2014 and August 2016.

In addition to extensive use of local labor, the project's Chinese contractor brought technical and managerial expertise to Ethiopia, contributing to its capability in infrastructure development.

卡洛特水电站

卡洛特水电站位于巴基斯坦北部印度河支流吉拉姆河上，距离首都伊斯兰堡的直线距离约55千米，装机容量72万千瓦，采用BOOT（建设—拥有—经营—转让）方式开发，总投资约17.4亿美元。电站建成后，每年可提供约32亿千瓦时的清洁电能，相当于巴基斯坦2017年全国水电发电总量的10%，将为巴基斯坦经济社会发展提供可靠的能源支持。该水电站是“一带一路”建设的首个水电项目，也是丝路基金2014年年底注册成立后投资的首个项目，同时还是“中巴经济走廊”优先实施的能源项目之一，更是迄今为止中国企业在海外投资在建的最大绿地水电项目。该项目已于2015年年底正式开工建设，预计2020年可以投入运营，运营期为30年，到期后无偿转让给巴基斯坦政府。除主要用于发电外，该项目还有防洪、拦沙、改善下游航运条件和发展库区通航等综合效益。项

Karot Hydropower Project

The Karot hydropower project is located on the Jhelum River, one of the rivers of the Indus River System in northern Pakistan, about 55 kilometers east of Islamabad. It is the first hydropower project implemented under the Belt and Road Initiative, and the first project financed by the Silk Road Fund since its inception in 2014. It is also one of the priority projects of the China-Pakistan Economic Corridor and the largest green field hydropower project ever undertaken overseas by a Chinese company.

The project is being developed on a build-own-operate-transfer basis. Started at the end of 2015, it is scheduled to be operational by 2020. After completion, it will be operated by the construction contractor for 30 years, after which the ownership will be transferred to the Pakistani government at no cost.

With an investment of US$1.74 billion, the power station will have an installed capacity of 720 MW and an average annual output of 3,200 Gwh, equivalent to 10 percent of Pakistan's total hydroelectric power generation in 2017. This will provide reliable energy support for economic and social development.

In addition to power generation, it will help flood prevention and sediment control, and improve downstream and reservoir area

目建设高峰期，可为当地提供超过2200个就业岗位，同时将带动当地电力配套行业的协调发展和产业升级。

transport services. The project is expected to create more than 2,200 new jobs during the construction period, and will spur coordinated and upgraded development in related sectors.

埃及苏伊士经贸合作区

埃及苏伊士经贸合作区是中国政府批准的第二批国家级境外经贸合作区，是集中了国家级资源开发建设的重点境外经贸合作区，始建于2008年，由“中非泰达投资股份有限公司”实施运营。合作区位于苏伊士湾西北经济区内，地处亚、非、欧三大洲交界的金三角地带，起步区面积1.34平方千米，目前累计投资约1亿美元，已基本开发完成。截至2015年年底，苏伊士合作区起步区共有企业68家，其中生产型企业达到了33家（含中资成分投资企业29家），另有生产、生活配套型企业35家。合作区累计吸引协议投资额超过9亿美元，现已初步形成了以宏华钻机和国际钻井材料制造公司为龙头的石油装备产业园区、以西电-EGEMAC高压设备公司为龙头的高低压电器产业园区、以中纺机无纺布为龙头的纺织服装产业园区、以巨石玻璃纤维公司为龙头的新型建材产业园区，以及以牧羊仓储公司为龙头的机械制造类产业园区在内的五大产业布局，并带动上、下游产业入区，快速形成产业集群效应。2014年9月，中埃双方签订了合作区扩展区项目，

Egypt Suez Economic and Trade Cooperation Zone

The Suez Economic and Trade Cooperation Zone is one of the second batch of state-level overseas economic and trade cooperation zones approved by the Chinese government. It is a key cooperation zone to be built with China's best resources. Construction started in 2008, and China-Africa TEDA Investment Co. Ltd. is the entity for the development.

Located in Egypt's Northwest Gulf of Suez Economic Zone in the triangle between Asia, Africa and Europe, the starting area covers 1.34 square kilometers. The initial development has been completed, with about US$100 million of investment.

By the end of 2015, 68 enterprises had settled in the starting area, including 33 manufacturing enterprises (29 Chinese-funded) and 35 service companies. It has absorbed over US$900 million of agreed investment. There are five industrial parks for different businesses: petroleum equipment manufacturing (Honghua Group), high and low voltage electric equipment (XD-EGEMAC High Voltage Electric Equipment Co.), textile and garments (China Textile Machinery Non-woven Fabrics Co.), new building materials (China Jushi fiberglass), and machinery

扩展区面积6平方千米，将分三期开发，开发建设总投资约2.3亿美元，根据扩展区建设开发规划，建成后的区域将吸引大约150－180家企业入驻，可以为埃及创造1万多个就业机会。2015年11月30日，中国泰达投资公司与埃方签署《苏伊士经贸合作区扩展区一期土地移交协议》，从埃方接受了一期2平方千米的土地。2016年1月习近平主席访问埃及期间，与塞西总统共同为扩展区揭牌。在埃及“苏伊士运河走廊开发计划”和共建“一带一路”倡议的推动下，合作区持续发展，在红海之滨的荒滩上建起一座现代化产业新城，成为中埃合作的重要成果。

manufacturing (Muyang Storage Engineering). Upstream and downstream industries have been attracted to produce cluster effects.

In September 2014, China and Egypt agreed to expand the zone by 6 square kilometers, which will be developed in three phases with a total investment of US$230 million. The expanded zone will accommodate 150-180 residential enterprises, and create more than 10,000 jobs for the Egyptians. On November 30, 2015, China's TEDA Investment Co. signed a land transfer agreement, by which it received two square kilometers of land from the Egyptian side. During his visit to Egypt in January 2016, Chinese President Xi Jinping unveiled the expansion zone together with Egyptian President Abdel Fattah al-Sisi.

Promoted by the Egyptian Suez Canal Corridor Development Plan and the Belt and Road Initiative, a modern industrial city is blossoming on the barren beach by the Red Sea, showcasing Sino-Egyptian cooperation.

图书在版编目（CIP）数据

中国关键词．“一带一路”篇：第2版：汉英对照/中国外文出版发行事业局，当代中国与世界研究院，中国翻译研究院著；韩清月，蔡力坚译．-- 北京：新世界出版社，2019.4（2023.3重印）

ISBN 978-7-5104-6737-0

Ⅰ．①中… Ⅱ．①中… ②当… ③中… ④韩… ⑤蔡… Ⅲ．①中国特色社会主义－社会主义建设模式－研究－汉、英②“一带一路”－国际合作－研究－汉、英 Ⅳ．① D616 ② F125.5

中国版本图书馆CIP数据核字(2019)第045971号

中国关键词：“一带一路”篇 第2版（汉英对照）

作　　者：中国外文出版发行事业局
当代中国与世界研究院　中国翻译研究院
翻　　译：韩清月　蔡力坚
审　　定：蔡力坚　徐明强
改　　稿：［英］David Ferguson
责任编辑：葛文聪
特约编辑：杨星宇
责任印制：王宝根
出　　版：新世界出版社
网　　址：http://www.nwp.com.cn
社　　址：北京西城区百万庄大街24号（100037）
发 行 部：(010) 6899 5968（电话）　(010) 6899 0635（电话）
总 编 室：(010) 6899 5424（电话）　(010) 6832 6679（传真）
版 权 部：+8610 6899 6306（电话）　nwpcd@sina.com（电邮）
印　　刷：天津中印联印务有限公司
经　　销：新华书店
开　　本：880mm × 1230mm　1/32
尺　　寸：95mm × 200mm
字　　数：120千字　印张：6.625
版　　次：2019年4月第1版　2023年3月第3次印刷
书　　号：ISBN 978-7-5104-6737-0
定　　价：68.00元

中国关键词

KEYWORDS TO UNDERSTAND CHINA

权 威 解 读 当 代 中 国

中国外文出版发行事业局（CICG）
中国翻译研究院（CATL）

新世界出版社
NEW WORLD PRESS

First Edition 2016

Compiled by China International Communications Group and China Academy of Translation
Translated by Han Qingyue
Cover Design by Yongcheng Tiandi

ISBN 978-7-5104-5938-2

Published by
NEW WORLD PRESS
24 Baiwanzhuang Street, Beijing 100037, China

Distributed by
NEW WORLD PRESS
24 Baiwanzhuang Street, Beijing 100037, China
Tel: 86-10-68995968
Fax: 86-10-68998705
Website: www.nwp.com.cn
E-mail: nwpcd@sina.com

Printed in the People's Republic of China

中国关键词（第一辑）图书编委会名单

Keywords to Understand China (I)

Editorial Committee

INTRODUCTION

前言

《中国关键词》（第一辑）多文版系列图书内容选编自“中国关键词多语对外传播平台”项目成果。

“中国关键词多语对外传播平台”是中国外文出版发行事业局和中国翻译研究院组织实施的国家重点项目，主要内容围绕以习近平同志为总书记的党中央治国理政新理念、新思想、新战略，进行中文词条专题编写、解读以及多语种编译，通过平面、网络和移动社交平台等多媒体、多渠道、多形态及时持续对外发布，旨在以国外受众易于阅读和理解的方式，阐释中国理念，解读中国思想、中国政策和中国发展道路。

《中国关键词》（第一辑）多文版系列图书所选词条是从“中国关键词多语对外传播平台”创建以来各文版发布的数百个词条中精选的部分内容，共计 9 册，包括英语、法语、俄语、西班牙语、阿拉伯语、德语、葡语、日语和韩语等 9 个语种，分 5 个专题，以中外文对照的方式呈现。

讲故事需要关键词，讲好中国故事需要中国关键词。让我们用“中国关键词”点击中国、沟通世界。

Keywords to Understand China (I) is a selection of the "China Keywords" entries included in an eponymous multilingual platform.

The "China Keywords" platform offers expert interpretation of the key governance philosophies of China's current CPC central leadership headed by Xi Jinping, and serves an international audience as a window into China's political thinking, policies, and path of development.

Undertaken by the China International Communications Group and China Academy of Translation, this national-level project provides timely updates in Chinese and nine foreign languages so far, and can be accessed online and on mobile social media platforms.

The highlights of the online "China Keywords" entries will be published in a multilingual book series *Keywords to Understand China*, and this is the first of the series with the entries arranged in five chapters and presented in Arabic, English, French, German, Japanese, Korean, Portuguese, Russian, and Spanish, in addition to Chinese explanation.

We hope that these "China Keywords" will help build a bridge of understanding between China and the rest of the world.

CONTENTS
目 录

综合篇 · General Topics

政治篇 · Political Development

经济篇 · Economic Development

外交篇 · Foreign Affairs

综合篇

General Topics

中国梦

实现中华民族伟大复兴，是中华民族近代以来最伟大的梦想，我们称之为“中国梦”，其基本内涵是实现国家富强、民族振兴、人民幸福。中国梦归根到底是人民的梦，人民对美好生活的向往就是中共的奋斗目标。实现中国梦，必须坚持中国道路、弘扬中国精神、凝聚中国力量。中国梦是和平、发展、合作、共赢的梦，不仅造福中国人民，而且造福世界人民。实现中国梦需要每一个中国人付出辛勤劳动和艰苦努力，实干才能梦想成真。

The Chinese Dream

Revitalizing the Chinese nation has been the greatest dream of the Chinese people since the beginning of modern times. It is called the Chinese Dream. It is a dream of prosperity, of national renewal, and of happiness. Fundamentally, it is a dream of the people, a yearning for a better life and a brighter future. And this is also what the Communist Party of China (CPC) has been striving for.

To make our dream come true, China must continue to follow the Chinese way of development, elevate the Chinese spirit, and boost national cohesion. Our dream is a dream of peace, development, cooperation and prosperity for all, benefiting not only the Chinese people but also the people of the rest of the world. Only by staying focused on achieving real results and making sustained, strenuous efforts can we bring our dream to fruition.

中国精神

中国精神的主要内涵就是以爱国主义为核心的民族精神，以改革创新为核心的时代精神。中国的爱国主义，并不是狭隘的民族主义，而是国际视野和国际胸怀的爱国主义。以改革创新为核心的时代精神，为中华民族实现中国梦提供强大的精神动力。

The Chinese Spirit

The Chinese spirit is the bedrock of our nation. It embodies patriotism and the courage to reform and to blaze new trails. Instead of bordering on narrow nationalism, our patriotism is informed by an international vision and a sense of inclusiveness. The courage to reform and to blaze new trails has provided a powerful impetus for our push to make the Chinese Dream come true.

中国特色社会主义

1982年，邓小平在中共十二大开幕词中指出“把马克思主义的普遍真理同我国的具体实际结合起来，走自己的路，建设有中国特色的社会主义”，第一次鲜明提出建设中国特色社会主义的重大命题。此后，建设中国特色社会主义就成为中国共产党全部理论和实践的鲜明主题。中国特色社会主义包含道路、理论体系和制度三个层面。道路是实现途径，理论体系是行动指南，制度是根本保障，三者统一于中国特色社会主义伟大实践上。中国特色社会主义，从理论和实践结合上系统回答了在中国这样人口多底子薄的东方大国建设什么样的社会主义、怎样建设社会主义这个根本问题。当前，建设中国特色社会主义，总依据是社会主义初级阶段，总布局是经济建设、政治建设、文化建设、社会建设、生态文明建设“五位一体”，总任务是实现社会主义现代化和中华民族伟大复兴。

Socialism with Chinese Characteristics

The concept of socialism with Chinese characteristics was first highlighted by Deng Xiaoping when he addressed the opening ceremony of the 12th National Congress of the Communist Party of China (CPC) in 1982. He emphasized the importance of integrating the universal truth of Marxism with China's realities, pursuing a path of our own, and building a socialist society with Chinese characteristics. Since then, this concept has been prominently embedded in the CPC's theoretical thinking and in all aspects of its work.

The concept consists of three pillars, namely our chosen path toward achieving our goals, a theoretical framework that offers guidance to action, and our political system that provides a fundamental basis to ensure that we proceed on the right track. All three pillars are integral to our great endeavor to build a socialist society with Chinese characteristics. By applying theoretical guidelines to practical needs, this concept provides a convincing answer to the central question: what type of socialism best suits the specific context of China, a large country with a huge population and a weak economic base, and how could we build such a socialist society?

The imperative to build socialism with Chinese characteristics is premised on the fact that China is in the primary stage of socialism. Our overall approach is to promote economic, political, cultural, social and ecological progress, while our overarching goals are to bring about socialist modernization and the great renewal of the Chinese nation.

中国特色社会主义的总依据

中国特色社会主义的总依据是社会主义初级阶段。社会主义初级阶段是当代中国的基本国情、基本实际。中国共产党和中国政府在任何情况下都要牢牢把握这个国情，推进任何方面的改革发展都要牢牢立足这个实际。不仅在经济建设中要始终立足初级阶段，而且在政治建设、文化建设、社会建设、生态文明建设中也要始终牢记初级阶段；不仅在经济总量低时要立足初级阶段，而且在经济总量提高后仍然要牢记初级阶段；不仅在谋划长远发展时要立足初级阶段，而且在日常工作中也要牢记初级阶段。

The General Premise of Socialism with Chinese Characteristics

Socialism with Chinese characteristics is premised on the fact that China is in the primary stage of socialism. All reform initiatives by the CPC and the Chinese government must be taken with due regard to present-day China's actual context. Efforts to promote economic, political, cultural, social and ecological progress must proceed on a clear understanding that China is still in the primary stage of socialism. Such an understanding should inform all aspects of our work, including long-term planning and day-to-day operations, even when our economic aggregates have shown clear improvement.

中国特色社会主义的总布局

中国特色社会主义的总布局是经济建设、政治建设、文化建设、社会建设、生态文明建设“五位一体”。中国特色社会主义是全面发展的社会主义，坚持以经济建设为中心，在经济不断发展的基础上，协调推进政治建设、文化建设、社会建设、生态文明建设以及其他各方面建设。

The Overall Approach to Building Socialism with Chinese Characteristics

Our overall approach to building socialism with Chinese characteristics is to promote economic, political, cultural, social and ecological progress. It is a holistic approach, with economic development as its central pillar and coordinated development in political, cultural, social, ecological and other areas pursued on the basis of continued economic growth.

中国特色社会主义的总任务

中国特色社会主义的总任务是实现社会主义现代化和中华民族伟大复兴。中国共产党从成立那天起，就肩负着实现中华民族伟大复兴的历史使命。中国共产党领导人民进行革命建设改革，就是要让中国人民富裕起来，国家强盛起来，振兴中华民族，按照现代化建设的战略部署，把中国建设成为富强民主文明和谐的社会主义现代化国家。

The Overarching Goals of Socialism with Chinese Characteristics

The overarching goals of socialism with Chinese characteristics are to bring about socialist modernization and the great renewal of the Chinese nation. Since its founding, the CPC has made it its historic mission to strive for national renewal. The objectives of revolutionary struggles, and economic development and reform efforts by the Chinese people under the leadership of the CPC have been none other than to secure a better life for the people, bring prosperity to the country, and bring about national renewal. Along the same lines, China's modernization strategy calls for building a modern socialist country that is prosperous, strong, democratic, culturally advanced and harmonious.

社会主义核心价值观

中共十八大提出，倡导富强、民主、文明、和谐，倡导自由、平等、公正、法治，倡导爱国、敬业、诚信、友善，积极培育和践行社会主义核心价值观。社会主义核心价值观明确了国家、社会、公民三个层面的价值目标、价值取向、价值准则，是对社会主义核心价值体系的高度凝练和集中表达，确立了当代中国最基本的价值观念。

The Core Values of Chinese Socialism

In November 2012 the 18th CPC National Congress called for efforts to foster the core values of the pursuit of prosperity, democracy, civility, harmony, freedom, equality, justice, rule of law, patriotism, dedication, integrity, and goodwill. These values define the goals, purposes, and norms of the state, society, and individual citizens, and reflect the true meaning of Chinese socialism and what we cherish and promote in contemporary China.

社会主义核心价值体系

2006年中共十六届六中全会提出建设社会主义核心价值体系，并指出社会主义核心价值体系包括四个方面的基本内容：马克思主义指导思想、中国特色社会主义共同理想、以爱国主义为核心的民族精神和以改革创新为核心的时代精神、社会主义荣辱观。

The System of Socialist Core Values

The system of socialist core values was introduced by the 16th CPC Central Committee at its sixth plenary session in October 2006. It encompasses the guiding principles of Marxism, the ideals of socialism with Chinese characteristics, the national spirit of patriotism, a commitment to reform and innovation, and a socialist honor code.

顶层设计

2010年10月18日，中国共产党十七届五中全会通过的《关于制定国民经济和社会发展第十二个五年规划的建议》提出“更加重视改革顶层设计和总体规划”。由此，“顶层设计”被引入中国的改革领域，并在此后一些中央文件和会议中进一步得到强调。“顶层设计”是中国重要的改革逻辑——由中央政府从全局的角度，系统地对改革任务进行统筹规划，调配资源，高效实现目标。

Top-Level Design

The Proposal on Developing the 12th Five-year Plan for National Economic and Social Development, adopted by the 17th CPC Central Committee at its fifth plenary session on October 18, 2010, introduced the idea of greater focus on designing at the top level and overall planning. The concept has subsequently been embedded in China's reform program and featured in other official documents and meetings of the central leadership.

"Top-level design" represents a key element of China's reform efforts. This means it is the central leadership that is responsible for devising a systematic overall plan for the nation's reforms from a strategic perspective, aiming to better allocate all the resources required and ensuring efficient realization of its goals.

“四个全面”

2014年12月，习近平在江苏省调研时，首次明确提出了“四个全面”战略布局，即全面建成小康社会、全面深化改革、全面依法治国、全面从严治党。

这四项工作是紧密联系在一起的：全面建成小康社会是中共十八大提出的总目标，全面深化改革与全面推进依法治国则如鸟之两翼，车之两轮，共同推动全面建成小康社会奋斗目标顺利实现。在这个过程中，全面从严治党则是各项工作顺利推进、各项目标顺利实现的根本保证。“四个全面”战略布局的提出，更完整地展现出中国新一届领导集体治国理政的总体框架。

The Four-Pronged Strategy

The Four-pronged Strategy was first put forth by Xi Jinping during an inspection tour of Jiangsu Province in December 2014. The strategy calls for completing the process of building a moderately well-off society, pursuing an all-round in-depth reform, implementing a comprehensive framework for promoting the rule of law, and launching an all-out effort to enforce strict Party discipline.

These four components of the strategy are mutually reinforcing. The completion of the process of building a moderately well-off society is the overall goal set by the CPC at its 18th National Congress. The pursuit of further reform and the promotion of the rule of law work side by side, like both wings of a bird or the two wheels of a chariot, to propel the country toward smooth realization of the goal. Efforts to strengthen Party discipline serve to ensure progress in all areas. The strategy provides an overall framework for the exercise of governance by China's new central leadership.

全面建成小康社会

“小康社会”是由邓小平在20世纪70年代末80年代初在规划中国经济社会发展蓝图时提出的战略构想。随着中国特色社会主义建设事业的深入，其内涵和意义不断地得到丰富和发展。在20世纪末基本实现“小康”的情况下，中共十六大报告明确提出了“全面建设小康社会”，中共十七大报告在此基础上提出新的更高要求，中共十八大报告根据我国经济社会发展实际和新的阶段性特征，在党的十六大、十七大确立的全面建设小康社会目标的基础上，提出了到2020年“全面建成小康社会”的目标。全面建成小康社会的目标主要包括：第一，转变经济发展方式取得重

Completing the Process of Building a Moderately Well-Off Society in All Aspects

The vision for a moderately well-off society was proposed by Deng Xiaoping in the late 1970s and early 1980s when the roadmap for China's economic and social development was being crafted. The concept has since been further enriched and developed in an evolving process of social-economic development with Chinese characteristics.

Considering the fact that the goal for a markedly improved life for the people had basically become a reality by the end of the 20th century, the CPC Central Committee called for a continued push to build a moderately well-off society in all aspects in its report to the 16th National Congress. New and more ambitious elements were subsequently added to this already expanded concept at the Party's 17th National Congress (held in 2007). In view of China's current status of and further needs for social-economic development, the CPC Central Committee announced in its report to the 18th National Congress the goal of completing the process of building a moderately well-off society in all aspects by the year 2020 on the basis of what had been achieved since the Party's previous two major gatherings.

大进展；第二，实现两个“倍增”，即国内生产总值和城乡居民人均收入比2010年翻一番；第三，通过增强创新驱动发展新动力，进入创新型国家行列；第四，工业化基本实现，信息化水平大幅提升，城镇化质量明显提高，农业现代化和社会主义新农村建设成效显著；第五，区域协调发展机制基本形成；第六，对外开放水平进一步提高，国际竞争力明显增强。

Specifically, the goal calls for: (a) making major progress in transforming China's growth model; (b) doubling China's 2010 GDP and per capita income for both urban and rural residents; (c) promoting innovation and pursuing innovation-driven development; (d) basically completing the process of industrialization, markedly expanding access to information technology, better managing urbanization, and making notable progress in agricultural modernization and rural development; (e) establishing a mechanism for development coordination across all regions; and (f) opening up further and notably improving China's international competitiveness.

全面深化改革

改革开放是决定当代中国命运的关键举措。2013年11月9日至12日召开的中共十八届三中全会审议通过并发布了《中共中央关于全面深化改革若干重大问题的决定》，提出了“全面深化改革”的新主张，为实施了三十多年的改革“升级”。2013年12月30日，中央全面深化改革领导小组成立。全面深化改革的总目标是：完善和发展中国特色社会主义制度，推进国家治理体系和治理能力现代化。它不是推进一个领域改革，也不是推进几个领域改革，而是涉及经济、政治、文化、社会、生态文明、国防和军队以及对外开放等所有领域改革；它不是单靠某一个或某几个部门，而是需要协调各方。全面深化改革的实现，需要进一步解放思想，紧紧依靠人民，加强和改善党的领导。在“四个全面”战略布局中，全面深化改革是重要动力。

An All-Round In-Depth Reform

The overall goal of our all-round push for further reform is to improve and develop the socialist system with Chinese characteristics and to modernize China's governance system and capabilities. The reforms will not be restricted to one or a few particular fields, but will involve a wide range of areas, including economic, political, cultural, social, and ecological policies, national defense, the military, and efforts to build a more open society. Success will not materialize with the efforts of one or a few particular departments, but will hinge on the concerted efforts of all sectors. Effective implementation of this new reform agenda entails further freeing our mind, reliance on the people, and strengthened and improved CPC leadership. An all-round push for further reform will be a key driver in the execution of China's Four-pronged Strategy.

全面依法治国

依法治国是中国共产党领导人民治理国家的基本方略。2014年10月20日至23日召开的中共十八届四中全会，作出了“全面推进依法治国”的新部署。它的总目标是：建设中国特色社会主义法治体系，建设社会主义法治国家。为实现这一目标，需要形成完备的法律规范体系、高效的法治实施体系、严密的法治监督体系、有力的法治保障体系，以及完善的党内法规体系。在全面推进依法治国进程中，要坚持依法治国、依法执政、依法行政共同推进，坚持法治国家、法治政府、法治社会一体建设，实现科学立法、严格执法、公正司法、全民守法。当前，中国面对的改革发展稳定任务之重前所未有，矛盾风险挑战之

A Comprehensive Framework for Promoting the Rule of Law

Promoting the rule of law is one of the fundamental pillars underpinning the CPC's national governance strategy that emphasizes the ownership role of the people. At its fourth plenary session held from October 20 to 23, 2014, the 18th CPC Central Committee rolled out a series of new initiatives to this end. The overall goal of these initiatives is to build the rule of law characteristic of Chinese socialism. To realize this goal it is vital to develop a sound legal system, buttressed by efficient and effective enforcement, oversight and support mechanisms, together with an effective intra-Party system of discipline and rules. The comprehensive process of promoting the rule of law should focus on ensuring that our Constitution and laws are fully complied with in national governance and in the exercise of political and executive power. Coordinated efforts should be made to strengthen our legal system and legal awareness throughout the country, at all levels of the government and in all sectors of society, so as to ensure the rationality of our legislative process, strict enforcement of and universal adherence to all laws, and impartial

多前所未有，比以往任何时候都更加需要运用法治思维和法治方式开展工作、解决问题，更好发挥法治的引领和规范作用。因此，全面依法治国是全面建成小康社会的迫切需要，也是全面深化改革、全面从严治党的迫切需要。

administration of justice. In view of the fact that China is currently faced with unprecedented challenges of moving forward with further reform, and ensuring development and stability, a rule-of-law culture has become more important than ever before in guiding our work and our thinking in approaching problems. Promoting the rule of law is therefore essential to realizing the country's goals of building a moderately well-off society and furthering reform, and to the CPC's efforts to strengthen discipline among its members.

全面从严治党

从严治党是中国共产党加强自身建设的一贯要求和优良传统。2014年12月，习近平总书记在江苏考察时，提出了“全面从严治党”的新要求，把管党治党提到前所未有的新高度。所谓“全面”，从内容上来说，就是要覆盖党的思想建设、组织建设、作风建设、反腐倡廉建设和制度建设这五个方面；从主体上来说，就是要覆盖到党的每一级组织、每一个党员。所谓“从严”，就是采用更严格的标准，对党员的要求比对普通民众的要求更严格，党的纪律要比其他团体更严明，党的规定要比一般法规更严格。它的重点在于从严管理监督党的干部。全面从严治党，是新一届中央领导集体治国理政的鲜明特征。它既是“四个全面”战略布局的重要组成部分，又在其中处于关键地位，是其他“三个全面”顺利推进的重要保证。

An All-Out Effort to Enforce Strict Party Discipline

Strict discipline has always been part of a great tradition of the CPC. While visiting Jiangsu Province in December 2014, Xi Jinping called for an all-out effort to enforce strict discipline, placing new emphasis on the importance of regulating the Party's own conduct.

An "all-out" effort is meant to cover the five cornerstones of Party development, namely theoretical development, organizational readjustment, work practices, anti-corruption campaigns, and institutional arrangements, and apply to every CPC organization and every CPC member. "Strict" discipline subjects CPC members to higher standards, i.e. standards more demanding than the general laws and regulations applicable to non-Party citizens. The focus is to provide restraints on Party members who hold official positions, and keep their activities under rigorous scrutiny.

An unwavering attention to strengthening Party discipline represents a defining feature of the current central leadership. As one of the components of the Four-pronged Strategy, the move to enforce discipline helps ensure progress in the other three areas.

“四个自信”

2016年7月1日，习近平总书记在庆祝中国共产党成立95周年大会上的讲话中，在“三个自信”（道路自信、理论自信、制度自信）基础上，增加了“文化自信”，从而形成了“四个自信”的表述。实际上，早在2014年2月，习近平在主持中央政治局集体学习时，就明确提出过“文化自信”的要求。2014年全国两会期间，他参加贵州代表团审议时说，“我们要坚持道路自信、理论自信、制度自信，最根本的还有一个文化自信”。

“四个自信”理念是对中国特色社会主义理论体系的丰富和创新。其中，道路自信是对中国特色社会主义道路发展方向和未来命运的自信；理论自信是对中国特色社会主义理论体系的科学性、真理性、正确性的自信；制度自信是对中国特色社会主义制度先进性和优越性的自信；文化自信是对中国自身文化价值的充分肯定，是对自身文化生命力的坚定信念，“是更基础、更广泛、更深厚的自信”。

Matters of Confidence

Addressing a grand meeting to celebrate the 95th anniversary of the founding of the CPC on July 1, 2016, Xi Jinping called on the whole Party to have confidence in its chosen path, guiding theories, and political system, and above all to have confidence in China's culture.

This was not the first time that Xi had emphasized the importance of cultural confidence. He had already raised the subject back in February 2014 when chairing a group study session of the Political Bureau of the CPC Central Committee. He referred to the topic again the following March when joining a discussion among NPC deputies from Guizhou Province. "We should have confidence in our chosen path, guiding theories, and political system, and most importantly, confidence in our culture," he told the deputies.

These "matters of confidence" can be seen to have developed and enriched the theories of socialism with Chinese characteristics. Confidence in the chosen path, offers a firm assurance about a promising future of Chinese socialism; confidence in the guiding theories affirms a strong belief that the theoretical framework of Chinese socialism is correct, scientific, and sound; confidence in the political system manifests an abiding faith in the strengths and advanced nature of Chinese socialism as a political system; confidence in China's culture demonstrates a full confirmation of the nation's own cultural values and a deep trust in their vitality. Such confidence is "more fundamental, more extensive, and more profound."

“四个自信”是一个有机统一体，是中国特色社会主义的完整信念体系，相辅相成、彼此互动。

Complementing each other and operating in harmony, these four matters of confidence constitute important components of Chinese socialism.

美丽中国

建设美丽中国是中国梦的重要内容。建设美丽中国，就是要按照尊重自然、顺应自然、保护自然的理念，贯彻节约资源和保护环境的基本国策，更加自觉地推动绿色发展、循环发展、低碳发展。建设美丽中国，就是要给自然留下更多修复空间，给农业留下更多良田，为子孙后代留下天蓝、地绿、水清的生产生活环境。中国梦的实现不以牺牲环境为代价，在发展经济的同时，保护好生态环境。建设“美丽中国”，有利于中国的长远发展，也将助推世界可持续发展，更有助于实现人类共同的梦想：保护美丽的地球。

Building a Beautiful China

Building a beautiful China is an important part of the Chinese Dream. It is an initiative that calls for respecting, protecting and being in harmony with nature, and is based on a key national policy on resource conservation, environmental protection, and promotion of green, circular and low-carbon development. It underscores the need for leaving more space for nature to renew itself, keeping more land for cultivation, and bequeathing a better working and living environment to future generations so that they could be blessed with a blue sky, green fields, and clean water. The Chinese Dream will not be realized at the expense of the environment. Economic development should be accompanied by strong measures of ecological protection. The initiative to build a beautiful China will be of benefit to the country's long-term development, to promoting sustainable global development, and to fulfilling the universal dream of protecting our beautiful earth.

党建篇

Party Building

民主集中制

民主集中制是中国国家政权的根本组织原则和领导原则。实行民主集中制，就是要求充分发扬民主，集体议事，使人民的意愿和要求得到充分表达和反映，在此基础上集中正确意见，集体决策，使人民的意愿和要求得以落实和满足。实行民主集中制，还要求“尊重多数，保护少数”，反对无政府主义的“大民主”，反对把个人意志凌驾于集体之上。民主集中制规定了领导和群众、上级和下级、部分和整体、组织和个人的正确关系，是维护党和国家团结统一、推进事业发展的重要保证。

Democratic Centralism

Democratic centralism is a fundamental principle that guides the exercise of organizational and leadership responsibilities in China's governance structure. It calls for a fully democratic process in collective deliberation that ensures the unrestricted expression of wishes and views of the people and the collection of useful ideas and suggestions. Decision-making is done collectively on the basis of such a process, so that people's expectations and needs can be satisfied. Democratic centralism also calls for respecting the opinions of the majority while protecting minority rights. It rejects anarchic democracy on the one hand and any tendency to allow the will of any individual to override collective wisdom on the other. It defines the relationship between officials and the public, between superiors and subordinates, between parts and the whole, and between organizations and individuals. Ultimately, it is vital for the unity of the CPC and the nation in furtherance of China's goals.

把权力关进制度的笼子里

在中国，一切权力都是人民赋予的，只能用来为人民谋利益。

把权力关进制度的笼子里，就是要加强对权力运行的制约和监督，形成不敢腐的惩戒机制、不能腐的防范机制、不易腐的保障机制。这三个机制实际上就是标本兼治、惩防并举的反腐倡廉体系的制度化标准。围绕三个机制建设，中国已建立纲纪严明的制度规范，让制度发挥其应有的作用。真正做到：任何人都没有法律之外的绝对权力，任何人行使权力都必须为人民服务、对人民负责并自觉接受人民监督。

Confining the Exercise of Power Within an Institutional Cage

All power in China is bestowed by the people and should be exercised only for the benefit of the people.

The move to confine the exercise of power within an institutional cage is meant to strengthen oversight of the work of the government and deter possible misuse of power by government officials. It entails establishing a mechanism that prevents, deters and punishes corruption. Such a mechanism should provide institutional firepower to fight corruption and promote integrity, by addressing both the symptoms and root causes of corruption with combined measures of punishment and prevention. To this end, China has established an effective framework of accountability with institutional checks on corruption. It is designed to ensure that no official enjoys absolute power above the law and that all officials exercise power to serve the people, are accountable to them and accept their oversight.

“打铁还需自身硬”

“打铁还需自身硬”，是中国流传已久的通俗名句，意思就是要从自己做起，以身作则，言传身教，率先垂范。2012年11月15日，中共中央总书记习近平在人民大会堂同采访十八大的中外记者见面时，提到了这句话。他引用这句中国俗语，意在强调加强中国共产党自身建设的重要性。中国共产党是执政党，把党建设好，是推进中国特色社会主义事业的关键。党坚强有力，事业才能兴旺发达，国家才能繁荣稳定，人民才能幸福安康。

"It takes a good blacksmith to make good steel."

"It takes a good blacksmith to make good steel" is a popular Chinese adage. It means that only by conducting yourself honorably can you expect others to do the same, or in other words, only a good example can serve as the best sermon. Xi Jinping quoted this saying when he met the press covering the 18th CPC National Congress at the Great Hall of the People on November 15, 2012 to explain the importance of Party building. The newly elected general secretary of the CPC Central Committee stressed that as the ruling party, the CPC must take a principled and disciplined approach to Party building, as this is the key to the advancement of socialism with Chinese characteristics. Only with a strong CPC, can there be progress towards our goals, prosperity and stability for our country, and happiness and peace for our people.

“三严三实”

“三严三实”是习近平对各级领导干部改进作风提出的要求，即严以修身、严以用权、严以律己，谋事要实、创业要实、做人要实。

严以修身，就是要加强党性修养，坚定理想信念，提升道德境界，追求高尚情操，自觉远离低级趣味，自觉抵制歪风邪气。严以用权，就是要坚持用权为民，按规则、按制度行使权力，把权力关进制度的笼子里，任何时候都不搞特权、不以权谋私。严以律己，就是要心存敬畏、勤于自省，遵守党纪国法。

The Three Guidelines for Ethical Behavior and the Three Basic Rules of Conduct

The initiative to implement the three guidelines for ethical behavior and the three basic rules of conduct (the 3+3 Initiative) was proposed by Xi Jinping. It calls upon officials at all levels to be strict with themselves in self-cultivation, in the exercise of power, and in self-discipline, and act in good faith when performing official duties, taking initiatives, and interacting with others.

Through self-cultivation officials are expected to enhance their awareness of the ethical standards of the Party, stand firm in support of its ideals and principles, cultivate integrity, pursue lofty goals, distance themselves from vulgar interests, and resist unhealthy practices and evil influences.

Prudence in the exercise of power emphasizes the importance of using power in the interests of the people, and in accordance with rules and regulations. Officials are expected to keep the exercise of power within the confines of institutional checks, and neither seek privileges nor abuse power for personal gain at any time.

Self-discipline promotes respect for the rule of law, diligence in self-examination, and strict adherence to Party discipline and state laws.

谋事要实，就是要从实际出发谋划事业和工作，使点子、政策、方案符合实际情况、符合客观规律、符合科学精神，不好高骛远，不脱离实际。创业要实，就是要脚踏实地、真抓实干，敢于担当责任，勇于直面矛盾，善于解决问题，努力创造经得起实践、人民、历史检验的实绩。做人要实，就是要做老实人、说老实话、干老实事。

Good faith in performing official duties entails due diligence in decision-making to ensure that all ideas, policies, and plans are context-appropriate, in line with actual conditions, and on well-conceived and rational basis. We should avoid being overly ambitious and divorced from reality.

Good faith in taking initiatives requires down-to-earth wisdom, results orientation, and accountability for our actions. We should be willing to face up to problems, and be adept at solving them, and strive to achieve real results that can stand the test of time.

Good faith in interacting with others calls for honesty in our daily life and work. We should always talk the talk, and walk the walk.

政治规矩

2015年1月13日，习近平总书记在十八届中央纪委第五次全会上的讲话中，正式提出了“政治规矩”一词。由此开始，这一概念迅速走进公众视野并受到广泛关注。对中共党员来说，“政治规矩”主要包括四方面内容：第一，党章是全党必须遵循的总章程，也是总规矩；第二，党的纪律是刚性约束，其中的政治纪律更是全党在政治方向、政治立场、政治言论、政治行动方面必须遵守的刚性约束；第三，国家法律是党员、干部必须遵守的规矩；第四，党在长期实践中形成的优良传统和工作惯例，也需要很好地遵守。领导人在当下重新提倡“政治规矩”，其主要目的是为了维护党中央权威，维护党内团结统一，重塑党组织的纪律性和约束力，净化党的政治生态。

Political Rules

Addressing the fifth plenary meeting of the Commission for Disciplinary Inspection of the 18th CPC Central Committee on January 13, 2015, Xi Jinping coined the term "political rules," which soon caught public attention.

The political rules applicable to CPC members include, *inter alia*:

- the Constitution of the Communist Party of China, which is the overriding statute that all members of the Party must observe;
- Party discipline, which is mandatory and binding, requiring all members of the Party to strictly abide by the guidelines and principles of the Party when making speeches or taking actions of a political nature;
- state laws, which exempts no CPC member or official;
- the great traditions and working practices developed by the Party over the years, which must be maintained.

These political rules are reiterated at this time against the backdrop of renewed attention to the need to ensure effective assertion of authority by the CPC Central Committee, maintain Party unity, reshape the Party's disciplinary practices and enforcement mechanism, and purify the Party's political ecosystem.

政治篇

Political Development

中国特色社会主义政治发展道路

中国特色社会主义政治发展道路，是中国共产党领导中国人民把马克思主义基本原理同中国具体国情相结合、经过长期探索实践逐步开辟和形成的。其关键是坚持党的领导、人民当家作主、依法治国有机统一，核心是坚持和完善人民代表大会制度、中国共产党领导的多党合作和政治协商制度、民族区域自治制度以及基层群众自治制度，目的是不断推进社会主义政治制度自我完善和发展。

Political Development Under Socialism with Chinese Characteristics

Political development under socialism with Chinese characteristics has evolved over time as the Chinese people made sustained efforts to build a better society under the leadership of the CPC by integrating the basic tenets of Marxism with China's specific conditions. The key features of such a process comprise leadership by the CPC, ownership by the people, and the rule of law. It is informed by continued efforts to improve the system of people's congresses, multiparty cooperation and political consultation under the leadership of the CPC, regional ethnic autonomy and community-level self-governance. Its objective is to continuously improve and develop the socialist political system.

人民代表大会制度

人民代表大会制度是中国人民当家作主的根本政治制度。人民通过全国人民代表大会和地方各级人民代表大会，行使国家权力。中国宪法规定：中华人民共和国全国人民代表大会是最高国家权力机关。在中国，国家行政机关、审判机关、检察机关都由人民代表大会产生，对它负责，受它监督。国家的重大事项由人民代表大会决定。行政机关负责执行人民代表大会通过的法律、决议、决定。法院、检察院依照法律规定分别独立行使审判权、检察权，不受行政机关、社会团体和个人的干涉。1954年9月，第一届全国人民代表大会第一次会议的召开，标志着人民代表大会制度在全国范围内正式建立。

The System of People's Congresses

Representing the fundamental core of China's political fabric, the system of people's congresses ensures that the people are the masters of the country. State power is exercised by the people through the National People's Congress (NPC) and local people's congresses. The preeminence of the NPC as the highest organ of state power is enshrined in China's Constitution. Heads of executive, judicial and procuratorial organs are elected or appointed by people's congresses, responsible to them and subject to their oversight. The decision-making on major public affairs is within the purview of people's congresses. The executive branch is responsible for implementing the laws, resolutions and decisions adopted by people's congresses. Courts and procuratorates exercise their respective judicial and procuratorial powers independently, free from the intervention of executive organs, social groups or individuals. The First Session of the First NPC, held in September 1954, marked the official establishment of the system of people's congresses nationwide.

中国共产党领导的多党合作和政治协商制度

中国的政党制度既不同于西方国家的两党或多党竞争制，也有别于一些国家实行的一党制，而是中国共产党领导的多党合作和政治协商制度。中国目前共有九个政党。除中国共产党外，还有中国国民党革命委员会（1948年成立）、中国民主同盟（1941年成立）、中国民主建国会（1945年成立）、中国民主促进会（1945年成立）、中国农工民主党（1930年成立）、中国致公党（1925年成立）、九三学社（1945年成立）、台湾民主自治同盟（1947年成立）。中国政党制度的显著特征是：中国共产党领导、多党派合作，中国共产党执政、多党派参政。各党派是与

Multiparty Cooperation and Political Consultation Under the Leadership of the Communist Party of China

China's political party system is different from two-party or multiparty systems of Western countries or one-party systems in some other countries. It is based on multiparty cooperation and political consultation under the leadership of the CPC. There are at present nine political parties in China. They are, in addition to the CPC, the Revolutionary Committee of the Chinese Kuomintang established in 1948, the Chinese Democratic League founded in 1941, the China National Democratic Construction Association founded in 1945, the China Association for Promoting Democracy established in 1945, the Chinese Peasants' and Workers' Democratic Party established in 1930, the China Zhi Gong Party founded in 1925, the Jiu San Society established in 1945, and the Taiwan Democratic Self-Government League established in 1947.

China's political party system is prominently characterized by the CPC's leadership role in governing the country with cooperation from and participation of all the other parties. Rather than being opposition parties or parties not in power, the other parties work closely with the CPC as partners and participate in government. They are involved

中国共产党团结合作的亲密友党和参政党，而不是反对党或在野党。各党派参加国家政权，参与国家大政方针和国家领导人选的协商，参与国家事务的管理，参与国家方针政策、法律法规的制定和执行。中国共产党坚持同各党派长期共存、互相监督、肝胆相照、荣辱与共。

in decision-making at all levels, consultations on national priorities and guidelines and the selection of candidates for state leadership positions, the management of state affairs, and the formulation and implementation of state policies, laws and regulations. The CPC always cherishes its long-time partnership with the other parties, a partnership reinforced by mutual oversight and mutual trust, and inspired by a shared desire to forge ahead together through thick or thin.

民族区域自治制度

中国是一个统一的多民族国家，迄今为止，通过识别并由中央政府确认的民族有56个。其中，汉族人口最多，其他55个民族人口较少，习惯上被称为少数民族。世界上的多民族国家在处理民族问题方面有不同的制度模式，中国采用的是民族区域自治。民族区域自治是在国家统一领导下，各少数民族聚居的地方设立自治机关，行使自治权，实行区域自治。民族区域自治制度是中国的一项基本政治制度。

1984年5月1日，中国颁布了《民族区域自治法》，把党和国家的民族区域自治政策法律化。2001年2月28日，又根据社会主义市场经济条件下出现的新情况，对这一法律进行修改，进一步确立了民族区域自治是中国一项基本政治制度的法律地位。目前，依据宪法和法律，中国共建立了155个民族自治地方，包括5个自治区、30个自治州、120个自治县（旗）。此外，还建立了1100多个民族乡。根据宪法和民族区域自治法的规定，民族自治地方拥有广泛的自治权。

Regional Ethnic Autonomy

China is a multiethnic country, a nation of 56 ethnic groups that have been recognized and confirmed by the central government. The Han ethnic group has the largest population, while the other 55 are minority ethnic groups with smaller populations. Compared with various different approaches to ethnic issues in other countries with multiethnic makeup, China's approach focuses on regional ethnic autonomy. Under the leadership of the central government, self-governance is exercised in regions with large ethnic minority populations, where local affairs are administered by local autonomous governing bodies. Regional ethnic autonomy is a basic component of China's political system.

The policies of the CPC and the central government on regional ethnic autonomy were later codified into law and promulgated on May 1, 1984 as the Law on Regional Ethnic Autonomy. The law was revised on February 28, 2001, in response to new developments associated with China's socialist market economy. The revised law further affirms regional ethnic autonomy as a basic component of China's political system. There are currently 155 ethnic autonomous areas in China designated in accordance with the Constitution and laws, including five autonomous regions, 30 autonomous prefectures, and 120 autonomous counties. There are also more than 1,100 ethnic townships. These autonomous regions, prefectures and counties enjoy extensive autonomy, as prescribed in the Constitution and the Law on Regional Ethnic Autonomy.

基层群众自治制度

随着中国的发展和进步，全国各地城乡基层民主不断扩大，公民有序地政治参与渠道增多，民主的实现形式日益丰富。目前，中国已经建立了以农村村民委员会、城市居民委员会和企业职工代表大会为主要内容的基层民主自治体系。广大人民在城乡基层群众性自治组织中，依法直接行使民主选举、民主决策、民主管理和民主监督的权利，对所在基层组织的公共事务和公益事业实行民主自治，已经成为当代中国最直接、最广泛的民主实践。截止到2012年11月，全国98%以上村委会实行直接选举，85%的村建立村民会议或村民代表会议制度，89%的社区建立居民代表大会。

Community-Level Self-Governance

China's increasing prosperity and progress have been accompanied by greater democracy at the community level in both urban and rural areas throughout the country, increased orderly participation of its citizens in political life, and a multiplication of democratic practices. Community-level democratic self-governance involves, *inter alia*, a network of rural villagers' committees, urban residents' committees and workers' congresses. Within these organizations people can directly participate in elections, policy-making, management and oversight. They are responsible for the public affairs and non-profit undertakings of their organizations. Community-level self-governance has become the most direct and extensive form of democracy in China today. As of November 2012, over 98 percent of China's villagers' committees had been elected directly; 85 percent of the villages had villagers' committees or congresses; and 89 percent of the urban communities had residents' congresses.

协商民主

人民通过选举、投票行使权利（即“选举民主”）和人民内部各方面在重大决策之前进行充分协商（即“协商民主”），尽可能就共同性问题取得一致意见，是中国社会主义民主的两种重要形式。社会主义协商民主是中国共产党和中国人民在社会主义民主形式方面的创造，符合中国的现实国情，契合中国的政治文化传统。它不仅关注最终的决策结果，也关注决策过程中的广泛参与，不仅强调对多数人意见的尊重，也强调少数人意见的充分表达和权利的维护，拓宽了民主的广度，从而在最大程度上实现人民民主。中国将不断推进协商民主广泛多层制度化发展，深入开展立法协商、行政协商、民主协商、参政协商、社会协商。

Consultative Democracy

China's socialist democracy finds expression in two processes: electoral democracy, which allows the people to exercise their rights through elections, and consultative democracy, which ensures that consultations are conducted with the people before major policy decisions are made. Both processes are designed to achieve the broadest possible consensus on issues of common concern. Socialist consultative democracy is a form of democracy developed by the CPC and the Chinese people by taking into account China's realities and its political and cultural traditions. It focuses not only on outcomes of decision-making but also on broad participation in this process. It emphasizes not only the importance of respecting the opinions of the majority, but also the need to ensure that minority voices are heard. It broadens the scope of democracy, so that people can enjoy democracy to the greatest extent possible. China will continue to develop an extensive, multilevel institutional framework for consultative democracy informed by wide-ranging deliberations on legislation, government programs, issues related to democracy, state affairs, and social issues.

统一战线

统一战线是中国共产党凝聚社会各方面力量，促进政党关系、民族关系、宗教关系、阶层关系、海内外同胞关系的和谐，夺取中国特色社会主义新胜利的重要法宝。新世纪新阶段，统一战线已经进一步发展成为全体社会主义劳动者、社会主义事业的建设者、拥护社会主义的爱国者和拥护祖国统一的爱国者的最广泛的联盟，具有空前的广泛性、巨大的包容性、鲜明的多样性和显著的社会性。推进中国特色社会主义事业，实现中华民族伟大复兴中国梦，必须巩固和发展最广泛的爱国统一战线，形成广泛、强大、持久的力量支持。

The United Front

The United Front is an essential tool that the CPC uses to pool the strength of the whole of Chinese society to build a prosperous socialist country with Chinese characteristics. It helps forge partnerships and build harmonious relations among political parties, among ethnic and religious groups, among different regions, and among people from all walks of life, including overseas Chinese. The United Front has further evolved in this new century into the broadest alliance of all actors who contribute to the socialist cause and patriots who support socialism or national reunification. It is characterized by its unrivaled reach, inclusiveness and diversity, and its strong commitment to social progress. To advance China's socialist cause and realize the Chinese Dream of national renewal, it is essential to strengthen and expand to the greatest extent possible the Patriotic United Front to bring about extensive, powerful and sustained support.

摸着石头过河

摸着石头过河，是富有中国特色、中国智慧、符合中国国情的改革方法。摸着石头过河就是摸规律。对于必须取得突破但一时还不那么有把握的改革，就先行试点，尊重实践、尊重创造，鼓励大胆探索、勇于开拓，取得经验、看得准了再推开。中国改革开放30多年来就是这样走过来的，是先试验、后总结、再推广不断积累的过程，是从农村到城市、从沿海到内地、从局部到整体不断深化的过程。这种渐进式改革，避免了因改革情况不明、举措不当而引起的社会动荡，为稳步推进改革、顺利

Crossing the River by Feeling for Stones

Crossing the river by feeling for stones is a distinctly Chinese approach to reform, one that embodies Chinese wisdom in addressing issues specific to contemporary China. It calls for prudence in feeling our way forward in unfamiliar territory, and testing the waters before a major course of action aiming at achieving breakthroughs is launched. It encourages innovation, exploration, and trailblazing efforts, while at the same time emphasizing the importance of identifying and promoting best practices on the basis of lessons learned.

This is how China's reform and opening up has proceeded in the past three decades. It has been a gradual process, starting with pilot programs, followed by larger campaigns to copy the successful experience to other places after a careful analysis of their outcomes. The process has spread from the countryside to the cities, from coastal areas

实现目标提供了保证。摸着石头过河，符合人们对客观规律的认识过程，符合事物从量变到质变的辩证法。不仅改革开放初期要摸着石头过河，现在全面深化改革同样还要摸着石头过河。当然，摸着石头过河也是有规则的，要按照已经认识到的规律来办，在实践中加深对规律的认识，也要在实践探索的基础上大胆突破，不能光摸石头不过河。

to the interior, and from localized projects to nationwide implementation. Such an incremental approach could help prevent potential social upheaval that could accompany an inappropriate major move resulting from lack of understanding of its implications. It ensures steady progress in moving ahead with our reform and in achieving our objectives.

Not only was this approach applicable to the initial phases of reform and opening up, it is also relevant in today's context when China is driving the reform to a deeper level. It should be applied judiciously, though. We should pursue our reform by taking into account what we have learnt from our past initiatives, and further deepen our understanding of what works and what does not, and blaze new trails on the basis of our new experience. Instead of simply feeling for stones, we should keep on moving forward to cross the river.

治大国若烹小鲜

“治大国若烹小鲜”一语出自中国古代思想家老子所著的《道德经》。意思是说治理大国，如同烹煮小鱼，关键在掌握好火候、调和好味道，而不可以不断翻搅。习近平主席2013年3月在接受巴西媒体采访时提出，领导者要深入了解复杂的国情和人民的多元需求，要有“如履薄冰，如临深渊”的自觉，以烹小鲜的态度治理社会，丝毫不敢懈怠，丝毫不敢马虎，必须夙夜在公、勤勉工作。

Governing a large state is like cooking a small fish: it must be handled with great care.

The adage "governing a large state is like cooking a small fish" came from *Daodejing* by Lao Zi, an ancient Chinese thinker. Just as cooking a small fish requires careful heat control, right seasoning, and a minimal amount of stirring, so governing a large state is a delicate balancing act that must be performed with the highest level of care. Responding to a question from a Brazilian reporter in March 2013, President Xi Jinping said that leaders must develop a clear understanding of the complexity of their country's realities and the diversified needs of their people. They must, he continued, be aware that governing a country is like "treading on thin ice or standing upon the edge of an abyss." It was essential, he added, to exercise extreme care and due diligence all the time in performing government functions in the same manner as we cook a small fish.

推进国家治理体系和治理能力现代化

这是中共十八届三中全会提出的全面深化改革的总目标之一。“国家治理体系和治理能力现代化”是一种全新的政治理念，表明中国共产党对社会政治发展规律有了新的认识，是马克思主义国家理论的重要创新，也是中国共产党从革命党转向执政党的重要理论标志。

国家治理体系就是在党领导下管理国家的制度体系，包括经济、政治、文化、社会、生态文明和党的建设等各领域体制机制、法律法规安排，是一整套紧密相连、相互协调的国家制度。

国家治理能力就是运用国家制度管理社会各方面事务的能力，包括改革发展稳定、内政外交国防、治党治国治军等各个方面。

Modernizing the National Governance System and Capabilities

One of the policy goals of an all-round in-depth reform set by the 18th CPC Central Committee at its third plenary session in November 2013 is to modernize the national governance system and capabilities. This is a new political concept that reflects the CPC's new understanding of the sociopolitical dynamics, and represents an important and innovative addition to the Marxist theory of the state. As a theoretical framework it also marks an important transition of the CPC from a revolutionary party to a party in power.

As China's institutional infrastructure under the leadership of the CPC, the national governance system comprises a full array of interlocking and mutually supplementary mechanisms that address economic, political, cultural, social, ecological, and Party-building issues, as well as legal and normative frameworks.

The national governance capabilities refer to the ability to use the national system to manage state affairs, including domestic and foreign affairs, and issues associated with reform, development, stability, and national defense, and to pursue efforts to build an exemplary Party, a prosperous country and a strong military.

推进国家治理体系和治理能力现代化，方向就是中国特色社会主义道路。要大力培育和弘扬社会主义核心价值体系和核心价值观，加快构建充分反映中国特色、民族特性、时代特征的价值体系。

The modernization of the national governance system and capabilities should follow the socialist path with Chinese characteristics. Efforts should be made to foster and promote the core values of Chinese socialism, and accelerate the building of a value system that fully captures what China is, what the Chinese nation stands for, and what our mission today calls for.

大道至简

在中国传统文化中，“大道至简”是指大道理（基本原理、方法和规律）是极其简单的，简单到一两句话就能说明白。中国总理李克强在2015年《政府工作报告》中提出“大道至简”，在此后的一次会议中他对此作出阐释，“简”来源于《论语 · 雍也》“居敬而行简”，“‘居敬’，就是我们作为公务人员，首先要在内心敬畏人民。‘行简’就是不要用太繁多的东西来扰民。”李克强认为，这与中国政府简政放权的理念是非常吻合的。

Great truths are always simple.

Great truths are always simple, as a saying goes in traditional Chinese culture. It means that fundamental principles, approaches and guiding rules are invariably straightforward and can be explained very concisely in simple words. Chinese Premier Li Keqiang quoted this saying in his Report on the Work of the Government to the National People's Congress in March 2015. In a subsequent meeting he further elaborated on it. The concept of simplicity, he said, comes from *The Analects* that advocates the virtue of holding the people in high regard and streamlining governance. In other words, we as civil servants must first of all treat the people with respect, and never harass them with too much red tape. This, he said, dovetails with our efforts at streamlining governance and decentralization.

简政放权

“简政”，即解决机构职能交叉、政出多门、人浮于事、相互掣肘的现象，解决社会公共产品和服务提供不足、行政效率低下的问题。“放权”，则是解决对经济活动审批过多、审批程序复杂、审批周期长效率低的问题，解决政府管了一些不该管的事情、一些该管的事情却没管好的问题。

中国本届政府把加快转变职能、简政放权作为开门第一件大事。到2013年底，分批取消和下放了416项行政审批等事项，2014年取消和下放审批事项200项以上。转变政府职能的核心要义，是要切实做好“放管”结合。“‘放’是放活，而不是放任；‘管’要管好，而不是管死。”

Streamlining Government and Delegating Authorities

Streamlining government aims at eliminating overstaffing and consolidating duplicate or overlapping – and often mutually interfering-government functions, so as to better address such problems as the inadequate provision of social public goods and services and the poor efficiency of the work of the government. Delegating authorities is intended to cut red tape that subjects an unnecessarily extensive array of business activities to a complex and lengthy government approval process. Such a move should free the government from unwarranted reach into areas it better stays away from to focus on what really falls within its purview, especially duties it is supposed to perform but has not performed adequately.

The current Chinese administration has made it a top priority to accelerate the process of transforming government functions, streamlining government and delegating authorities. By the end of 2013, a total of 416 items originally requiring State Council review and approval had been reclassified as exempt from such review or sent to lower levels of the government for approval. More than 200 items were addressed in a similar manner in 2014. The key to transforming government functions is a right balance between delegation and

简政放权是为了理顺政府与市场的关系，更好地发挥市场在资源配置中的作用，归根结底是促改革调结构惠民生。由事前审批变为事中事后监管，不是给政府工作“减压”，而是相关工作要做得更细致，监管要更到位。这种工作方式的转变，对政府职能部门提出了更高的要求：不仅观念要变，更要增长能力，要主动研究市场规律，具备前瞻眼光，对市场发展有利的要积极鼓励，对市场发展不利的要及时调整。

the exercise of control. To delegate authorities is meant to inject more vitality into economic activities, rather than embracing an unqualified *laissez-faire* approach. To exercise control is to ensure that the market functions appropriately, rather than stifling the economy with regulatory overreach.

The initiative to streamline government and delegate authorities helps rationalize the relationship between the government and the market, giving the market a bigger role to play in allocating resources. This ultimately propels reform, helps restructuring and improves people's well-being. The shifting of focus from pre-implementation approval to monitoring during and after project implementation calls for a more detail-oriented and better targeted supervisory function for the government, instead of reducing its workload. Such a change represents a challenge for government departments. There is now a need for a paradigm shift and enhanced capacity-building. It is vital to develop a forward-looking vision and be proactive in gauging market dynamics with a view on amplifying the positive effect of market drivers and minimizing the negative influence of any market failure in a timely manner.

转变政府职能

转变政府职能是深化行政体制改革的核心，它实质上要解决政府应该做什么、不应该做什么，重点是明析政府、市场、社会的关系，即哪些事应该由市场、社会、政府各自分担，哪些事应该由三者共同承担。总体上看，改革开放以来，中国各级政府在转变政府职能方面取得了重大成就，积累了宝贵经验，有力推进了社会主义现代化建设。但现在政府职能转变还不到位，政府对微观经济运行干预过多过细，宏观经济调节还不完善，市场监管问题较多，社会管理亟待加强，公共服务比较薄弱，必须下更大决心、更大力度推进政府职能转变，以更好适应深化改革开放、加快转变经济发展方式、转变工作作风、维护社会和谐稳定的迫切要求。

Transforming Government Functions

Transforming government functions is at the core of a more in-depth administrative structural reform drive. Essentially it involves determining what the government should do and should not do, by clarifying the roles of the government, the market and society, i.e., clearly defining what should be dealt with by each of them individually or jointly.

Generally speaking, since the reform and opening-up policy was introduced in the late 1970s, great progress has been made in transforming the functions of the governments at all levels, and valuable experience gained, providing strong impetus to the country's modernization process.

However, much remains to be done in this respect. Government intervention in the micro-economy is still considered excessive and too intrusive. It is also imperative to improve macro-economic regulation, and address inadequacies in market regulation, and social and public services. With greater resolve, we must intensify our push for transforming government functions. Only by so doing, can we better meet the pressing challenges to drive the process of reform and opening up to a deeper level, speed up the transformation of the growth model, encourage ethical conduct, and maintain social harmony and stability.

让权力在阳光下运行

权力不论大小，只要不受制约和监督，都可能被滥用。让权力在阳光下运行，就是要健全权力运行制约和监督体系，让人民监督权力，确保国家机关按照法定权限和程序行使权力。要强化制约，合理分解和配置权力，不同性质的权力由不同部门、单位、个人行使，形成合理的权力结构和运行机制。要强化监督，着力改进对领导干部特别是一把手行使权力的监督，加强领导班子内部监督，加强行政监察、审计监督、巡视监督。纪委派驻监督要对党和国家机关全覆盖，巡

Greater Transparency in the Exercise of Power

Power is susceptible to abuse at all levels if it is not subject to constraints and oversight.

Greater transparency in the exercise of power requires an improved system of checks and balances, and greater participation of the people in monitoring the way in which authority is used, so as to ensure that government departments and agencies exercise power within their respective mandates and in accordance with procedural requirements. In addition to more constraints on power, it entails rational separation and distribution of powers. It is important to put in place a sound system and implementation mechanisms through which different functions are performed by different government departments, agencies or individuals. Oversight should be stepped up, and the performance of government functions, particularly by those who hold top positions at all levels, should be placed under more rigorous scrutiny. Internal oversight should also be strengthened, and so should administrative supervision, auditing and onsite inspections.

视监督要对地方、部门、企事业单位全覆盖。要强化公开，推行地方各级政府及其工作部门权力清单制度，依法公开权力运行流程，让权力在阳光下运行，让人们监督，保证权力正确行使。增强权力制约和监督效果，还必须保证各级纪委监督权的相对独立性和权威性。

The presence of commissions for discipline inspection should be extended to all Party and state bodies, and onsite inspections should cover all government departments, state enterprises and public institutions nationwide. To increase transparency, a complete list of powers should be established for governments at all levels and their functional departments, and procedures for exercising power made public in accordance with the law. Oversight by the people is essential to ensuring greater accountability and appropriate exercise of public authority. Any move to strengthen checks and balances and oversight must be accompanied by measures to ensure the independence and authority of commissions for discipline inspection in performing their duties.

网络强国战略

网络强国战略是中国为实现由网络大国到网络强国而拟定的国家发展战略。2014年2月，习近平总书记提出了努力把中国建设成为网络强国的战略目标，并从掌握互联网核心科技、建设健康网络文化、完善信息基础设施、加强互联网人才队伍建设、开展互联网国际合作等方面，对如何建设网络强国提出了明确的要求。中共十八届五中全会将网络强国战略纳入“十三五”规划的战略体系，提出实施网络强国战略，从战略高度和顶层设计的角度进一步明确了建设“网络强国”的国家战略，这显示出中国领导人对信息化、网络化和现代化、全球化趋势的深刻理解和把握。“十三五”期间，中国将以技术创新助推强国战略，以网络文化根植强国战略，以基础设施牢筑强国战略，以网络安全和信息化护航强国战略，以国际合作提升强国战略，向着网络基础设施基本普及、自主创新能力显著增强、信息经济全面发展、网络安全保障有力的目标不断前进。

The "Internet Power" Strategy

The "Internet Power" strategy aims to put China, a country with an extensive cyber presence, on track to an Internet technology leader. The strategy was proposed by Xi Jinping in February 2014. It calls for developing core Internet technologies, promoting a healthy cyber culture, strengthening IT infrastructure, improving talent management, and expanding Internet-related international cooperation.

At its fifth plenary session in October 2015, the 18th CPC Central Committee incorporated the "Internet Power" strategy into the 13th Five-year Plan, further clarifying its strategic importance. This move was prompted by a growing understanding of the imperatives to pursue the development of information technology and the Internet and modernization, and the trends of globalization.

Under the 13th Five-year Plan (2016-2020), China will step up efforts to encourage technological innovation, build a healthy cyber culture, strengthen infrastructure and cyber security, increase the use of information technology, and expand international cooperation as part of its "Internet Power" strategy. The goal is to provide easy access to IT infrastructure, enhance innovation, bolster the information economy, and ensure cyber security.

军民融合战略

2015年3月，习近平出席十二届全国人大三次会议解放军代表团全体会议时提出，“把军民融合发展上升为国家战略”；同年10月的中共十八届五中全会上明确提出，“实施军民融合发展战略，形成全要素、多领域、高效益的军民深度融合发展格局”。这被认为是中国长期探索经济建设和国防建设协调发展规律的重大成果。实施军民融合发展战略，关键在于统筹经济建设和国防建设，使经济建设与国防建设相互促进、相互支撑，实现富国和强军的统一。为了实施好该战略，“十三五”期间，中国一方面将在国家层面加强顶层设计，把国防和军队建设规划的宏观需求纳入经济社会发展规划，并完善配套政策法规制度，加大法规建设力度。另一方面也将引入竞争激发活力，打破军工垄断体制、降低民企准入门槛、强化安全保密监管，确保资源投入有质量有效益。

The National Military-Civilian Integration Strategy

Addressing the plenary session of the military delegates to the Third Session of the 12th National People's Congress in March 2015, Xi Jinping announced a plan to step up military-civilian integration as part of a national strategy. At its fifth plenary session in October 2015 the 18th CPC Central Committee decided to implement such a strategy to build an extensive and efficient multi-sector structure for integrating military and civilian resources. This was seen as a major step toward strengthened coordination between economic growth and military development.

The key to effectively implementing the strategy is a high level of integration of economic and national defense priorities to create synergy so that efforts on both fronts become complementary to each other and mutually reinforcing. During the period covered by the 13th Five-year Plan (2016-2020), planning at the top level will be intensified to incorporate national defense and military needs into an overall economic and social development framework. At the same time related regulatory policies and legal mechanisms will be fine-tuned. It is also necessary to introduce competition into the defense industry by breaking the monopoly of defense enterprises and improving market access for civilian businesses, while guaranteeing security, confidentiality, quality and cost-effectiveness.

中国人民抗日战争胜利纪念日

中国人民抗日战争胜利纪念日是指中国为纪念抗日战争胜利确定的国家纪念日。1951年8月13日，中央人民政府政务院发布通告，将抗战胜利纪念日确定为9月3日。2014年2月27日，中国第十二届全国人大常委会第七次会议经表决通过了将9月3日确定为中国人民抗日战争胜利纪念日的决定，以国家立法的形式再次确认。2014年9月3日，中国党和国家领导人习近平、李克强、张德江、俞正声、刘云山、王岐山、张高丽等出席了在中国抗日战争纪念馆举行的首个纪念活动。2015年9月3日，为纪念中国人民抗日战争暨世界反法西斯战争胜利70周年，中国举行了包括阅兵式在内的隆重的纪念活动，共有来自49个国家的政府首脑及代表出席了阅兵式等纪念活动。

The Victory Day of the Chinese People's War of Resistance Against Japanese Aggression

The Victory Day of the Chinese People's War of Resistance Against Japanese Aggression is the day designated for celebrating China's victory over Japan. In a circular of August 13, 1951, the Government Administration Council of the Central People's Government of China declared September 3 as China's Victory Day. This designation was reaffirmed by the Standing Committee of the 12th National People's Congress of China in a legislative decision adopted at its seventh session on February 27, 2014. Top Chinese leaders, including Xi Jinping, Li Keqiang, Zhang Dejiang, Yu Zhengsheng, Liu Yunshan, Wang Qishan, and Zhang Gaoli, attended a commemoration ceremony at the Museum of the War of Chinese People's Resistance Against Japanese Aggression on September 3, 2014. A grand celebration, including a military parade, was held on September 3, 2015 to mark the 70th anniversary of victory of the Chinese people's resistance against Japanese aggression and the world anti-fascist war. Heads of state or government and representatives from 49 countries attended the military pageantry and other commemorative activities.

以国家立法的形式确立纪念日并举行纪念和悼念活动，表明中国人民反对侵略战争、捍卫人类尊严、维护世界和平的坚定立场。同时，也是为了警醒全世界人民时刻警惕日本军国主义死灰复燃，避免历史悲剧的重演，更好地维护世界和平。

By designating through a legislative act a day for commemorating its victory, China has shown to the world that the Chinese people are determined to stand firm against any war of aggression and in defense of human dignity and world peace. The annual commemorative activities are also a reminder that the world should always be on guard against the resurgence of Japanese militarism and a possible replay of historical tragedies, so as to better safeguard world peace.

“九二共识”

“九二共识”的缘起是为实现和推进两岸协商奠定政治基础。1992年10月底至12月初，中国大陆的民间团体——海峡两岸关系协会与台湾的民间团体——海峡交流基金会，经过多次磋商，最终形成了以口头方式表达的“海峡两岸均坚持一个中国的原则”的共识，后被称为“九二共识”。其核心是“坚持一个中国”，精髓是求同存异。“九二共识”明确界定了两岸关系的性质，即大陆与台湾同属一个中国，两岸关系不是国与国关系，也不是“一中一台”。“九二共识”是两岸关系保持和平稳定和良性互动的基础。正是以“九二共识”为基础，才实现了2005年4月在北京举行的国共两党领导人历史性会谈，以及2015年11月在新加坡举行的两岸领导人历史性会晤。

"1992 Consensus"

The "1992 Consensus" was an oral agreement reached between the mainland-based Association for Relations Across the Taiwan Straits (ARATS) and the Taiwan-based Straits Exchange Foundation (SEF) as a result of their talks held from late October to early December of 1992. The two non-governmental organizations agreed that "both sides of the Taiwan Straits will follow the one-China principle," which subsequently became the political foundation for cross-Straits consultations.

The kernel of the "1992 Consensus" is the "one-China principle," which means seeking common ground while reserving differences. The "1992 Consensus" defines cross-Straits relations as neither state-to-state nor "one China, one Taiwan," but confirms the fact that the mainland and Taiwan belong to one China.

The "1992 Consensus" is the foundation on which cross-Straits relations can progress in peace and stability and with positive interactions. It was on this basis that the historical discussions of the leaders of the CPC and the KMT were conducted in Beijing in April 2005, and the historical meeting between the leaders from both sides of the Taiwan Straits was held in Singapore in November 2015.

习马会

两岸领导人习近平、马英九于2015年11月7日在新加坡会面，就进一步推进两岸关系和平发展交换意见。这是1949年以来两岸领导人的首次会面。双方在会面时就推进两岸关系和平发展达成积极共识：肯定2008年以来两岸关系和平发展取得的重要成果。认为应该继续坚持"九二共识"，巩固共同政治基础，推动两岸关系和平发展，维护台海和平稳定，加强沟通对话，扩大两岸交流，深化彼此合作，实现互利共赢，造福两岸民众。此次会面，翻开了两岸关系历史性的一页。

The Xi-Ma Meeting

On November 7, 2015, Xi Jinping and Ma Ying-jeou, leaders from both sides of the Taiwan Straits, met in Singapore to exchange views on furthering the peaceful development of cross-Straits relations. This was a historic meeting, the first since 1949, of the leaders from both sides of the Taiwan Straits.

Both sides acknowledged the progress that has been made in cross-Straits relations and peaceful development since 2008. They reaffirmed their commitment to the "1992 Consensus" and a number of other key commitments: to consolidating common political ground, maintaining peace and stability in the development of cross-Straits relations, increasing communication and dialogue, and expanding exchanges and cooperation to the benefit of people in both Chinese mainland and Taiwan. This meeting opened a new chapter in the history of cross-Straits relations.

经济篇

Economic Development

“两个一百年”奋斗目标

中共十八大描绘了全面建成小康社会、加快推进社会主义现代化的宏伟蓝图，发出了向“两个一百年”奋斗目标前进的时代号召。该奋斗目标是，到2021年中国共产党成立一百年时全面建成小康社会，国内生产总值和城乡居民人均收入比2010年翻一番；到2049年中华人民共和国成立一百年时建成富强民主文明和谐的社会主义现代化国家，达到中等发达国家水平。“两个一百年”奋斗目标，将中国梦的宏伟蓝图和光明前景具体化。实现“两个一百年”奋斗目标是实现中国梦的基础。

The Two Centennial Goals

At its 18th National Congress the CPC presented a roadmap and issued a call for achieving the Two Centennial Goals: successfully completing the process of building a moderately well-off society; and accelerating socialist modernization. Specifically, this means doubling China's 2010 GDP and per capita income for both urban and rural residents by the time the CPC celebrates its centenary in 2021, and building China into a modern socialist country that is prosperous, strong, democratic, culturally advanced, and harmonious and reaches the level of moderately developed countries by the time the People's Republic of China celebrates its centenary in 2049. The Two Centennial Goals embody the grand vision and ambitious ideals the Chinese Dream represents, and achieving these goals will provide the basis for making the Chinese Dream a reality.

中国经济新常态

中国经济新常态的三个主要特点：一是从高速增长转为中高速增长。二是经济结构不断优化升级，城乡区域差距逐步缩小，居民收入占比上升，发展成果惠及更广大民众。三是从要素驱动、投资驱动转向创新驱动。

新常态给中国带来的影响主要包括：经济增速虽然放缓，实际增量依然可观；经济增长更趋平稳，增长动力更为多元；经济结构优化升级，发展前景更加稳定；中国政府大力简政放权，市场活力进一步释放。

The New Normal of China's Economy

The new normal of China's economy is characterized by: (a) a shift from high growth rates to medium-high growth rates; (b) an on-going process of optimizing and upgrading the economic structure, and narrowing the urban-rural gap, with higher personal income as a share of GDP, and an increasing number of people benefiting from economic development; and (c) a transition from growth driven by factors and investment to one driven by innovation.

This new normal would likely lead to, among others, a sizable increase in real output despite slower growth; more stable growth with a more diversified array of growth drivers; an increasingly optimized and upgraded economic structure, and more predictable development prospects; and a further revitalized market as result of the on-going move to streamline government and delegate authorities.

“四个没有变”

2015年7月17日，习近平在吉林长春召开座谈会时，就中国经济形势做出了“四个没有变”的归纳。此后的11月18日，他在出席亚太经合组织工商领导人峰会时，再次强调了“四个没有变”，即：中国经济发展长期向好的基本面没有变，经济韧性好、潜力足、回旋余地大的基本特征没有变，经济持续增长的良好支撑基础和条件没有变，经济结构调整优化的前进态势没有变。“四个没有变”的判断，揭示了中国经济发展的基本态势和未来趋势，表明中国有信心、有能力保持经济中高速增长，赢得了国内外的普遍认可。

The Four Features of China's Economic Conditions That Remain Unchanged

During a symposium in Jilin Province on July 17, 2015, Xi Jinping pointed out that four features of China's economic conditions remain unchanged. On November 18 of the same year, at the APEC CEO Summit, he once again spoke on this topic. These features are:

- China's positive economic fundamentals and long-term trajectory;
- the basic characteristics of strong resilience, great potential, and ample room for maneuver;
- strong support and conditions favorable for continued growth;
- positive progress in structural adjustment and upgrading of the economy.

This assessment confirms the current basic conditions and future trends of economic growth in China, and shows its confidence in maintaining a medium-high rate of growth and its ability to do so.

改革开放

改革开放是中国共产党历史上的一次觉醒，是决定当代中国命运的关键举措，也是决定实现“两个一百年”奋斗目标、实现中华民族伟大复兴的关键举措。改革开放永无止境，只有进行时，没有完成时。

1978年12月，中国共产党召开了具有重大历史意义的十一届三中全会，开启了对内改革、对外开放的历史新时期。其目的就是要解放和发展生产力，实现国家现代化，让中国人民富裕起来。中国改革开放最主要的成果是开创和发展了中国特色社会主义，中国的面貌、中国与世界的关系都发生了深刻的变化。中国实现了从高度集中的计划经济体制到充满活力的社会主义市场经济体制、从封闭半封闭到全方位开放的伟大历史转折。中国经济持续30年保持10%以上的增长速度，经济总量已经位居世界第二。中国解决了13亿人的温饱问题，为世界贫困人口减少的贡献超过70%。截止到2015年，中国城镇居民人均可支配收入由343元增长到31195多元；农民人均纯收入由133元增长到11422元，人民生活总体上

Reform and Opening Up

The process of reform and opening up was propelled by a new awakening of the CPC. It has been key to making China what it is today, and will be essential to realizing the Two Centennial Goals and national renewal. It is an on-going process with no end point.

The process that ushered in a new historical period was initiated in 1978 when the 11th CPC Central Committee held its third plenary session. Aimed at dismantling the economic straitjacket and unlocking the growth potential, the reform program put China on the path to modernization and prosperity.

In addition to the emergence and development of the concept of socialism with Chinese characteristics, the achievements of China's reform and opening up are most convincingly demonstrated by the profound changes it has brought to China and to its relations with the rest of the world.

China has made the historic shift from a centrally planned economy to a dynamic socialist market economy and from a closed or semi-closed society to an open one. With an annual growth rate of more than 10 percent for 30 years running, China has become the second largest economy in the world. The challenge to provide its 1.3 billion people with adequate food and everyday essentials has been successfully addressed, contributing to a 70 percent reduction in the number of people living in poverty worldwide. With the per capita disposable

达到小康水平。中国主动适应并积极参与世界格局变革调整进程，以负责任大国形象展现在世人面前。2015年，根据国际货币基金组织公布的数据，中国经济对全球经济增长的贡献率超过25%。中国依靠自己的力量实现了经济社会转型，没有发生对外战争、海外殖民和大规模的社会动荡，政治体制保持稳定，法治化程度不断提升，社会生活的自由度不断扩大，民众对政府的信任度接近90%。

income of China's urban residents increasing from RMB 343 to over RMB 31,195, and the per capita net income of its farmers rising from RMB 133 to more than RMB 11,422, the goal of building a moderately well-off society has been largely achieved.

China is also adapting to an evolving world landscape, and actively participates in global affairs as a responsible member of the international community. It now accounts for nearly 25 percent of world economic growth. It has brought about economic and social transformation without getting involved in wars on foreign lands, pursuing overseas colonization, or causing widespread social unrest. It has enjoyed political stability, strengthened rule of law, and expanded individual freedom. The public's trust in government is near 90 percent.

市场在资源配置中起决定性作用

2013年11月召开的中共十八届三中全会提出，要让市场在资源配置中起决定性作用。市场决定资源配置是市场经济的一般规律，健全社会主义市场经济体制必须遵循这条规律，着力解决市场体系不完善、政府干预过多和监管不到位问题，推动资源配置依据市场机制实现效益最大化和效率最优化。做出“使市场在资源配置中起决定性作用”的定位，有利于在全党全社会树立关于政府和市场关系的正确观念，有利于转变经济发展方式，有利于转变政府职能，有利于抑制消极腐败现象。当然，发展社会主义市场经济，既

The Decisive Role of the Market in Resource Allocation

The market should play a decisive role in resource allocation, according to a decision by the 18th CPC Central Committee at its third plenary session in November 2013. A general rule embraced by market economies, the preeminence of the market in allocating resources should also be a feature of our socialist market economy. To this end efforts should include building a robust market, and rolling back excessive government intervention while also addressing insufficient government oversight in some areas, so as to promote the market's role in maximizing the effectiveness and efficiency in resource allocation.

This decision would guide the Party and the general public in developing a new, appropriate perspective for the relative roles of the government and the market. It would also help transform the growth model and government functions, and rein in corruption and other forms of misconduct.

要发挥市场作用，也要发挥政府作用，但市场作用和政府作用的职能是不同的。更好发挥政府作用，就要科学宏观调控，健全宏观调控体系、全面正确履行政府职能、优化政府组织结构，加强和优化公共服务，保障公平竞争，加强市场监管，维护市场秩序，推动可持续发展，促进共同富裕，弥补市场失灵，保持宏观经济稳定。

While there is no doubt that the development of a socialist market economy entails contributions from both the market and the government, their specific functions are different. The performance of the government could be improved by sound macroeconomic regulation, a better macro-control system, and full implementation of reasonably-defined government functions, with optimized government organizational structures and strengthened public services. It is also crucial to ensure fair competition, enhance market oversight to maintain order, address market failures when need arises to maintain macroeconomic stability, and promote sustainable development and prosperity for all.

发挥经济体制改革的牵引作用

中共十八届三中全会决定描绘的全面深化改革的路线图中，突出强调以经济体制改革为重点，发挥经济体制改革牵引作用。这是因为，中国仍处于并将长期处于社会主义初级阶段的基本国情没有变，人民日益增长的物质文化需要同落后的社会生产之间的这一社会主要矛盾没有变，中国是世界最大发展中国家的国际地位没有变。这就决定了经济建设仍然是中心工作。坚持以经济建设为中心不动摇，就必须坚持以经济体制改革为重点不动摇。当前，制约科学发展的体制机制障碍不少集中在经济领域，经济体制改革任务远远没有完成，经济体制改革的潜力还没有充分释放出来。经济基础决定上层建筑，经济体制改革对其他方面改革具有重要影响和传导作用，重大经济体制改革的进度决定着其他方面很多体制改革的进度，具有牵一发而动全身的作用。在全

Economic Structural Reform – an Engine of Progress

The roadmap for implementing an all-round in-depth reform presented by the 18th CPC Central Committee at its third plenary session highlights the role of economic structural reform as an engine of progress. This is necessitated by the fact that China is still in the primary stage of socialism and will remain so for a long time to come. Our larger context remains basically unchanged. The growing material and cultural needs of the people still outpace productivity growth. China remains the world's largest developing country. Against such a backdrop China has to keep economic development as its central task. In so doing, it must stay focused on economic structural reform. At present, many institutional and structural deficiencies constraining balanced development are found in the economic sphere. There is a long way to go before we accomplish the task of economic structural reform, and its potential has yet to be fully unleashed.

The economic basis determines the superstructure, and economic structural reform has an important impact on, and helps propel, reforms in other fields. The progress of major economic reform initiatives is key to progress in many other structural reform efforts, and indeed has a direct bearing on all that is at stake.

面深化改革中，我们要坚持以经济体制改革为主轴，努力在重要领域和关键环节改革上取得新突破，以此牵引和带动其他领域改革，使各方面改革协同推进、形成合力，而不是各自为政、分散用力。

Economic structural reform remains the central pillar of our all-round in-depth reform efforts. Major new progress must be made in key areas of this reform, so as to pave the way for, and provide impetus to, other sectorial reforms. Such an approach could ensure synergy and coordination between various reform initiatives, and avoid silo mentality and fragmentation.

转方式、调结构、稳增长

自“十二五规划”（2011-2015）以来，“转方式、调结构、稳增长”一直是中国宏观经济及各部门各地区的重要政策目标。转方式，就是推动经济发展方式由粗放型增长到集约型增长，从低级经济结构到高级、优化的经济结构，从单纯的经济增长到全面协调可持续的经济发展的转变。调结构，就是通过调整国民经济各组成部分的地位和相互比例关系，使其更加合理化、高级化，适应并促进生产力的发展。稳增长就是坚持扩大内需、稳定外需，大力发展实体经济，努力克服各种不稳定不确定因素的影响，保持经济平稳运行。

Growth Model Transformation, Structural Adjustments, and Steady Growth

Since the rollout of China's 12th Five-year Plan for National Economic and Social Development (2011-2015), a major policy goal has been to transform the growth model and make structural adjustments while ensuring steady growth at the national, regional and sectorial levels.

Growth model transformation calls for replacing extensive growth with intensive growth, upgrading and optimizing economic structure, and pursuing growth that is comprehensive, balanced, and sustainable rather than purely economic.

Structural adjustments involve realigning and rationalizing various components of the economy, in order to adapt to new dynamics and boost productivity.

Steady growth entails expanding domestic consumption, maintaining steady overseas demand, developing the real economy, and addressing the root causes of instability and uncertainty.

五大发展理念

2015年10月26日至29日在北京召开的十八届五中全会，首次提出了“创新、协调、绿色、开放、共享”的五大发展理念。该理念强调，要把创新摆在国家发展全局的核心位置，要正确处理发展中的重大关系，要坚持节约资源和保护环境的基本国策，要奉行互利共赢的开放战略，坚持发展为了人民、发展依靠人民、发展成果由人民共享，等等。五大发展理念的提出，集中反映了中国共产党对经济社会发展规律认识的深化，为中国共产党带领全国人民全面建成小康社会提供了有力的思想指导。

Five Concepts for Development

At its fifth plenary session held from October 26 to 29, 2015, the 18th CPC Central Committee called for "development that is innovation-driven, coordinated, green, oriented toward global progress, and beneficial to all." Of these five concepts for development, innovation should be given top priority, while interactions between all the individual fields must be properly managed. The basic state policy of resource conservation and environmental protection should be respected, as should the principle that opening to the world must be to the benefit of all parties involved. Development should be in the interests of the people, rely on their support, and be of direct benefit to them. The thinking behind the five concepts for development embodies the CPC's in-depth understanding of the laws of economic and social development, while the concepts offer a theoretical guideline for the leadership in building a moderately well-off society in all respects.

创新发展

作为“五大发展理念”之一，创新发展注重的是解决中国发展的动力问题。中国领导人把创新作为引领发展的第一动力，期望以此实现从要素驱动转向创新驱动、从依赖规模扩张转向提高质量效益，加快形成以创新为主要引领和支撑的经济体系和发展模式。“十三五”期间，中国将把发展基点放在创新上，增强自主创新能力，并从培育发展新动力、拓展发展新空间、深入实施创新驱动发展战略、大力推进农业现代化、构建产业新体系、构建发展新体制、创新和完善宏观调控方式等七个着力点，绘制、实施创新发展的路线图。

Innovation-Driven Development

As one of the five concepts for development put forward by China's leadership, innovation-driven development focuses on what drives China's development. Considered the most critical growth driver, innovation should be encouraged so as to propel the country's transition from an input-driven economy to one driven by innovation, and from relying on expansion of scale to increasing efficiency. Efforts should be made to accelerate the process of building a development model for an economy driven and sustained by innovation.

During the 13th Five-year Plan (2016-2020) period, China will rely on innovation to boost its growth and reinforce its creativity. It will foster new driving forces, and expand the space for development in its implementation of the strategy of innovation-driven development. Modernization of agriculture will proceed full steam ahead, together with initiatives to build a new economic structure and a new institutional base that facilitates development, and encourage innovative improvements in macro-regulation.

协调发展

作为“五大发展理念”之一，协调发展注重的是解决中国发展中的不平衡问题。中国以往高速发展过程中出现和积累的不平衡、不协调、不可持续问题，已经成为继续发展的“短板”。“十三五”期间，中国将会增强发展协调性，其重点有三：促进城乡区域协调发展，旨在破解城乡二元结构难题；促进经济社会协调发展，旨在改变“一条腿长、一条腿短”失衡问题；促进新型工业化、信息化、城镇化、农业现代化同步发展，致力于在增强国家硬实力的同时注重提升国家软实力，增强发展整体性。

Coordinated Development

Coordinated development is the second of China's five concepts for development. In tandem with China's high-speed growth, problems of imbalance and unsustainable development have begun to emerge, becoming points of weakness that hinder its further development. The 13th Five-year Plan (2016-2020) envisions strengthened policy coordination aimed at (a) promoting coordinated urban and rural development, so as to overcome the usual urban-rural dichotomy; (b) facilitating coordinated economic and social development, so as to bridge the gap currently existing between the two processes, and (c) synchronizing its new model of industrialization with efforts at expanding access to information technology, urbanization, and agricultural modernization. It is essential to integrate development efforts in different areas in a seamless manner that helps upgrade China's hard and soft power.

绿色发展

作为“五大发展理念”之一，绿色发展注重的是解决人与自然和谐相处的问题。“十三五”期间，中国将遵循绿色发展理念，在促进人与自然和谐共生，加快建设主体功能区，推动低碳循环发展，全面节约和高效利用资源，加大环境治理力度，筑牢生态安全屏障等六个方面下功夫，推动建立绿色低碳循环发展产业体系，致力于把生态文明建设融入经济、政治、文化、社会建设的各方面和全过程，以期让中华大地青山常在、绿水长流、蓝天永驻。

Green Development

As one of the five development concepts, green development highlights the importance of harmony between man and nature. Under the 13th Five-year Plan (2016-2020), heightened attention will be given to an eco-friendly approach to development in order to preserve harmony between man and nature. The process of designating functional regions will be accelerated. Efforts will be stepped up to promote low-carbon and circular development, conservation and efficient utilization of resources, and environmental protection, and safeguard China's ecological security. It is imperative to build an economic structure conducive to green, low-carbon and circular development, and incorporate an eco-conservation perspective into every facet of economic, political, cultural, and social development. Our goal is: the land we inherit will remain blessed with green mountains, clear waters, and fresh air.

开放发展

作为“五大发展理念”之一，开放发展注重的是解决中国发展内外联动的问题。中国从六个方面对开放发展进行了部署：完善对外开放战略布局，形成对外开放新体制，推进“一带一路”建设，深化内地和港澳、大陆和台湾地区合作发展，积极参与全球经济治理，积极承担国际责任和义务。这显示出深度融入世界的中国期望以开放发展实现合作共赢，有效促进中国和世界的共同发展。

Development for Global Progress

The fourth component of the conceptual framework for development, development for global progress focuses on interactions between China and the rest of the world.

The following six areas of action are highlighted in the 13th Five-year Plan (2016-2020):

- improving the strategic planning of the process of opening up;
- creating a new mechanism for this purpose;
- promoting the Belt and Road Initiative;
- increasing cooperation between the mainland and Hong Kong, Macao, and Taiwan;
- playing a more active role in global economic governance; and
- taking on greater international responsibilities and obligations.

Through closer interactions with the rest of the world, China wishes to effectively promote global progress through cooperation beneficial to all.

共享发展

作为“五大发展理念”之一，共享发展注重的是解决社会公平正义问题。让人民群众共享改革发展成果，是社会主义的本质要求，是社会主义制度优越性的集中体现，也是中国共产党坚持全心全意为人民服务根本宗旨的必然选择。共享发展的明确指向，在于促进公平正义，实现人的全面发展。中国就共享发展作出增加公共服务供给、实施脱贫攻坚工程、提高教育质量、促进就业创业、缩小收入差距、建立更加公平更可持续的社会保障制度、推进健康中国建设、促进人口均衡发展等八个方面的部署。这既是有效的制度安排，也是中国“十三五”期间推动共享发展的重要着力点。

Development for the Benefit of All

Development for the benefit of all, the fifth of China's five concepts for development, is aimed at promoting social equity and justice. Ensuring universal enjoyment of the fruits of reform and development is what our socialist ideals call for, and most aptly reflects the advantages of our socialist system. It also embodies the ultimate goal of the Communist Party of China to whole-heartedly serve the people.

Development for the benefit of all is about empowering the people to reach their full potential in an enabling environment conducive to safeguarding equity and justice. The 13th Five-year Plan (2016-2020) lists the following measures to this end:

- expanding access to public services;
- effectively implementing poverty-alleviation projects;
- improving the quality of education;
- creating more jobs and encouraging new businesses;
- narrowing the income gap;
- building a more equitable and sustainable social security system;
- improving healthcare services; and
- promoting balanced population growth.

打好扶贫攻坚战

改革开放30多年来，中国经济社会发展取得很大成就，人民生活水平总体上发生很大变化，几亿贫困人口脱贫，完成这期间全世界超过70%的减贫任务。但由于中国还处在社会主义初级阶段，由于国家大、各地发展条件不同，中国还有为数不少的困难群众，扶贫开发依然任重道远。按照农民年人均纯收入2300元的扶贫标准，到2015年底，中国农村贫困人口还有5575万人。可见，中国扶贫的工作已经进入"啃硬骨头"阶段。这种背景下，从2014年开始，中国将每年10月17日设立为"扶贫日"。中国将加大投入力度，动员社会各方面力量共同向贫困宣战，深入推进扶贫开发，继续打好扶贫攻坚战，帮助困难群众早日脱贫致富，稳定实现扶贫对象不愁吃、不愁穿，保障其义务教育、基本医疗、住房，努力推动贫困地区经济社会加快发展。

Alleviating Poverty

Since China introduced the policy of reform and opening up in the late 1970s, great economic and social progress has been made, leading to significant improvement in the overall standards of living. As a result, several hundred million people have been lifted out of poverty, accounting for more than 70 percent of poverty reduction worldwide during the same period. Much remains to be done, however, to eliminate the still substantial pockets of poverty, given the fact that China, a country with a large population, is still in the primary stage of socialism, and its diverse regions show varying levels of development.

At the end of 2015 China's 55.75 million rural residents still lived below the national poverty line, that is, having an annual net income of less than RMB 2,300 per capita. China's poverty alleviation initiatives are now facing some of the most daunting challenges.

Against such a backdrop, China launched in 2014 its first National Poverty Alleviation Day, which is to be marked on October 17 each year. China will allocate more resources for poverty relief and mobilize all sectors of society to join the fight against poverty. Development efforts aimed specifically at reducing poverty will be stepped up, so as to put an early end to poverty. Effective measures will be implemented to steadily improve access to adequate food and daily necessities, compulsory education, basic medical services and housing.

精准扶贫、精准脱贫

2014年12月11日闭幕的中国中央经济工作会议，首次在中央工作层面明确提出了精准脱贫的概念；2015年6月18日，习近平在贵州调研时强调，扶贫开发“贵在精准，重在精准，成败之举在于精准”，“精准扶贫”随后成为社会各界热议的关键词。2015年11月3日发布的“十三五规划建议”中，进一步作出“实施精准扶贫、精准脱贫”的工作部署。精准脱贫，就是要防止用经济收入的平均数掩盖大多数，更加注重保障基本民生，更加关注低收入群众生活。精准扶贫，则是要做到对贫困人口进行精确识别、精确帮扶，对扶贫工作做到精确管理。中央明确提出精准扶贫、精准脱贫，是因为中国的扶贫开发工作已进入“啃硬骨头、攻坚拔寨”的冲刺期。为了真正实现“精准”目标，习近平提出了“扶贫对象精准、措施到户精准、项目安排精准、资金使用精准、因村派人精准、脱贫成效精准”的具体要求。

Targeted Approach to Alleviating Poverty

At the closure of the Central Economic Work Meeting on December 11, 2014, the central leadership floated the idea of a targeted approach to alleviating poverty. On June 18, 2015, during his visit to Guizhou Province, Xi Jinping once again raised the subject, which he believes will determine the success of the poverty alleviation drive. It has subsequently become a hot topic among the general public. In its Proposal for Formulating the 13th Five-year Plan for National Economic and Social Development, released in November 2015, the 18th CPC Central Committee specified targeted measures to be taken in the coming five years.

Targeted efforts are designed to ensure that average income statistics would not eclipse the true living conditions of many in hardship. Such efforts require attention to detail. Greater emphasis will be laid upon identifying low-income groups in need of assistance, so that they will receive due attention and their basic standard of living will be guaranteed.

The central leadership proposed such a targeted approach at a time when China faces a daunting challenge in its efforts to eliminate the final pockets of poverty across the country. To ensure that poverty reduction efforts are fully effective, Xi Jinping called for policies and programs of assistance to be tailored for the needs of individual families in conjunction with targeted funding and village-specific expert support, and to be pursued with a results-oriented focus.

生态红线

生态红线，亦称生态保护红线，是指在自然生态服务功能、环境质量安全、自然资源利用等方面，需要实行严格保护的空间边界与管理限值，以维护国家和区域生态安全及经济社会可持续发展、保障人民群众健康。

生态红线是国家生态安全的底线和生命线，这个红线不能突破，一旦突破后果必将危及生态安全、人民生产生活和国家可持续发展。

中国政府正在通过精心研究和论证，确定究竟哪些要列入生态红线，如何从制度上保障生态红线，把良好生态环境尽可能保护起来。生态红线一旦确立，全国就要一体遵行，决不能逾越。

Ecological Red Lines

Ecological red lines, also known as "ecological conservation red lines," refer to space boundaries and environmental management limits that must be strictly observed in ecological conservation services, environmental quality and safety controls, and natural resources utilization in order to ensure national and regional ecological safety, sustainable economic and social development, and people's health.

These lines are essential for securing China's ecological safety, and must not be crossed. Otherwise the country's ecological safety, people's working and living conditions, and sustainable development will all be endangered.

The Chinese government is conducting research to delineate the red lines and provide institutional guarantees, so as to offer the best possible protection for a healthy environment. Once the mechanism of red lines is in place, it must be implemented throughout the country without fail.

生态补偿制度

中共十八届三中全会《决定》提出实行生态补偿制度。生态补偿制度，是以防止生态环境破坏、增强和促进生态系统良性发展为目的，以从事对生态环境产生或可能产生影响的生产、经营、开发、利用者为对象，以生态环境整治及恢复为主要内容，以经济调节为手段，以法律为保障的新型环境管理制度。它可分为广义和狭义两种。广义包括对污染环境的补偿和对生态功能的补偿，狭义则专指对生态功能或生态价值的补偿。中国政府将坚持谁污染环境、谁破坏生态谁付费和谁受益谁补偿原则，完善对重点生态功能区的生态补偿机制，推动地区间建立横向生态补偿制度。

Eco-Compensation System

The decision to establish an eco-compensation system was made by the 18th CPC Central Committee at its third plenary session. The system aims at preventing damage to the environment, and enhancing and promoting ecological conservation and protection. It targets those involved in business and other activities, including production, and exploitation and use of natural resources, that have or might have negative environmental impacts. It represents a new approach to environmental stewardship that relies on market-based mechanisms and a legal framework to promote protection and restoration of ecosystem services.

The eco-compensation approach can be understood in both a broad and a narrow sense. Broadly speaking, it involves compensation for environmental pollution or for damage to ecosystem functions. In a narrow sense, it refers specifically to compensation for damage to ecosystem functions and their values.

The Chinese government will implement the "polluter pays" principle to make those responsible for producing pollution and benefiting therefrom responsible for paying for the damage done to the environment. Efforts will be stepped up to improve the compensation mechanism for key ecosystem function conservation areas and to establish cross-regional eco-compensation programs.

战略性新兴产业

所谓战略性新兴产业，是指那些潜在市场大、带动能力强、吸收就业多、综合效益好的产业，比如节能环保、新一代信息技术、高端装备制造、集成电路、物联网、先进制造、新能源、新一代移动通信、大数据等。中国将适应产业竞争格局新变化，加快培育这些产业发展，构建“核心技术—战略产品—工程与规模应用”的创新价值链，拓展产业发展空间，培育市场竞争新优势。

Emerging Industries of Strategic Importance

Emerging industries of strategic importance are those that have considerable market potential, can drive the economy and create more jobs, and are cost-effective. They include energy conservation and environmental protection, new-generation information technology, high-end equipment manufacturing, integrated circuits, the Internet of Things, advanced manufacturing, new energy, new-generation mobile communications, and big data.

China will step up efforts to foster the growth of these industries in response to new challenges in a competitive world. An innovative value chain will be created linking core technologies, strategic products, and engineering expertise and capacity and large-scaled applications. The scope of industrial development will be expanded, with new possibilities for businesses to sharpen their competitive edge.

创新驱动发展战略

中国实施创新驱动发展战略，就是要推动以科技创新为核心的全面创新，坚持需求导向和产业化方向，坚持企业在创新中的主体地位，发挥市场在资源配置中的决定性作用和社会主义制度优势，增强科技进步对经济增长的贡献度，形成新的增长动力源泉，推动经济持续健康发展。主要措施包括：营造激励创新的公平竞争环境，建立技术创新市场导向机制，强化金融创新的功能，完善成果转化激励政策，构建更加高效的科研体系，创新培养、用好和吸引人才机制，推动形成深度融合的开放创新局面，等等。中国将力争到2020年，基本形成适应创新驱动发展要求的制度环境和政策法律体系，为进入创新型国家行列提供有力保障。

The Innovation-Driven Development Strategy

China's innovation-driven development strategy aims at encouraging innovation in all areas, particularly scientific and technological innovation. Innovation should be demand-driven in response to the needs of industrialization. Businesses are major players in delivering innovation, and the market should play the decisive role in allocating resources. The full potential of our socialist system should be explored. The strategy seeks to enhance the contribution of scientific and technological advances to economic growth, which would serve as a new growth driver and help sustain sound economic development.

The main measures to be taken to this end include creating a favorable environment for fair competition and a market-based mechanism that encourages technological innovation. It is also essential to promote financial innovation to provide more incentives for innovative uses of technology. Another area of focus is building a more efficient scientific research system, and implementing an effective talent management mechanism for training and attracting competent personnel. A highly integrated approach is necessary to ensure an open, innovation-friendly climate. China seeks to have in place by 2020 an institutional, legal and policy framework for innovation-driven development so as to provide a solid basis to put China on track to one of the world's most innovative countries.

大众创业、万众创新

习近平在2014年12月的中央经济工作会议上提出要“营造有利于大众创业、市场主体创新的政策制度环境”。此前，李克强在2014年9月的夏季达沃斯论坛上也曾提出，要掀起“大众创业”“草根创业”的新浪潮，形成“万众创新”“人人创新”的新态势。“大众创业、万众创新”是实现中国经济提质增效升级的“新引擎”，其目的在于尊重人民群众的主体地位，充分发挥其无限创造力，让他们平等参与现代化进程、共同分享改革红利和发展成果。推动大众创业、万众创新，可以扩大就业、增加居民收入，有利于促进社会纵向流动和公平正义，同时也可以让中国民众在创造财富的过程中，更好地实现精神追求和自身价值。

Widespread Entrepreneurship and Innovation

At the Central Economic Work Meeting in December 2014, Chinese President Xi Jinping called for efforts to create at policy and institutional levels an environment conducive to widespread entrepreneurship and innovation. Before that, Premier Li Keqiang had declared at the "Summer Davos" forum in Tianjin in September that China would encourage widest possible participation in entrepreneurial activities and help unleash a massive wave of grassroots innovation.

Widespread entrepreneurship and innovation would be a new engine for China to upgrade the economy, making it more efficient. The axiom testifies to the leading role of the people and the need to tap into their unbounded creativity in full participation in China's drive towards modernization and enjoyment of the reform dividend and the fruits of development. Promoting entrepreneurship and innovation would create more jobs, increase people's income, boost social mobility, and contribute to social equity and justice. This would in turn encourage individuals to further pursue their ideals and realize their full potential while generating higher levels of wealth.

新型城镇化道路

在中国这样一个拥有13亿人口的发展中大国实现城镇化，在人类发展史上没有先例。粗放扩张、人地失衡、举债度日、破坏环境的老路不能再走了，也走不通了。在这样一个十分关键的路口，必须走出一条新型城镇化道路，切实把握正确的方向。

新型城镇化道路是从社会主义初级阶段基本国情出发，遵循规律，因势利导，使城镇化成为一个顺势而为、水到渠成的发展过程。

坚持把城镇化质量明显提高摆在突出位置来落实。坚持以人为本，推进以人为核心的城镇化；坚持优化布局，促进大中小城市和小城镇合理分工、功能互补、协同发展；坚持生态文明，着力推进绿色发展、循环发展、低碳发展；坚持传承文化，发展有历史记忆、地域特色、民族特点的美丽城镇。

A New Path to Urbanization

Never in history has a developing country as large as China, with a population of 1.3 billion, attempted to engineer a carefully managed urbanization. China can no longer follow the beaten track of inefficient and blinkered development relying on borrowed money that damages the environment and results in an imbalance between the needs of the population and land resources. That path will lead the country nowhere. At this crossroads, China must take a new path to urbanization in the right direction.

The new urbanization drive is based on China's realities in the primary stage of socialism. It is a choice that meets our development imperatives and enables us to make the best use of the opportunities available to bring assured success to this process.

Emphasis should be put on achieving the best results of urbanization. A people-centered approach is indispensable. Appropriate plans should be worked out to ensure that towns and cities of all sizes complement each other with well-defined functions for coordinated development. Eco-friendly measures will be effectively implemented in our push for green, circular and low-carbon development. Special care must be taken to preserve traditional culture in our effort to redevelop cities and towns with historical landmarks and local or ethnic features.

“供给侧改革”

2015年11月20日，在中央财经领导小组第十一次会议上，习近平首次提出了“供给侧改革”这一重要理念。“供给侧”是相对于“需求侧”而言的，它是从供给和生产端入手，通过鼓励企业创新、促进淘汰落后、化解过剩产能、降低税费负担等方式，解放生产力、提升竞争力，从而促进经济发展。“供给侧改革”更加注重经济结构的优化，核心在于提高全要素生产率，政策手段包括简政放权、放松管制、金融改革、国企改革、土地改革、提高创新能力等。“供给侧改革”的提出，旨在加大结构性改革力度，进一步释放内需潜力、激发供给活力，以创新供给带动需求扩展，以扩大有效需求倒逼供给升级，实现稳增长和调结构互为支撑、互促共进。

Supply-Side Reform

The importance of "supply-side reform" was emphasized by Xi Jinping at the 11th meeting of the CPC Central Leading Group for Financial and Economic Affairs on November 10, 2015. Supply-side policies, which focus on supply and production, are often discussed in contrast to a demand-side approach. To improve supply-side performance is to unleash productivity and maintain a competitive edge, with greater innovation, decommissioning of obsolete manufacturing, less overcapacity, and lower tax rates, so as to boost economic growth.

This reform is placing greater emphasis on optimizing the economic structure and enhancing the efficiency of all contributing factors. To this end, measures will be implemented to streamline government and delegate powers, relax macro-regulation, spur innovation, and reform the financial sector, land use rights, and SOEs. The reform plan is designed to accelerate structural change, fuel domestic demand and expand supply. Innovation will be encouraged to generate greater demand, which will in return lead to improvements in supply. Steady growth and structural adjustment should be mutually supportive and proceed in parallel.

"中国制造2025"

2015年5月8日，中国国务院正式印发《中国制造2025》，成为中国实施制造强国战略第一个十年的行动纲领。文件中透露，"中国制造2025"的总体思路是，坚持走中国特色新型工业化道路，以促进制造业创新发展为主题，以加快新一代信息技术与制造业深度融合为主线，以推进智能制造为主攻方向，强化工业基础能力，提高综合集成水平，完善多层次人才体系，实现中国制造业由大变强的历史跨越。

它的目标是：到2020年，基本实现工业化，制造业大国地位进一步巩固，制造业信息化水平大幅提升；到2025年，制造业整体素质大幅提升，创新能力显著增强，全员劳动生产率明显提高，工业化和信息化融合迈上新台阶。"中国制造2025"的实施，也将会为世界各国带来更多的合作机遇，共同推动制造业整体向前发展。

Made in China 2025

On May 8, 2015, China's State Council unveiled its first 10-year national plan for transforming China's manufacturing, entitled "Made in China 2025." The plan is designed to put China on a new path to industrialization, with greater emphasis on innovation, expanded use of new-generation information technology, intelligent manufacturing, consolidation of the industrial base, integration of industrial processes and systems, and a robust multilayer talent development structure. Measures taken in this respect will facilitate China's transformation from a manufacturing giant with a focus on quantity to one with a qualitative edge.

Specifically, the ten-year plan envisions the successful completion by 2020 of the process of basic industrialization, further consolidating China's position as a manufacturing powerhouse that increasingly relies on cutting-edge information technology. It also foresees a significant leap in China's overall manufacturing capability by 2025, characterized by markedly reinforced innovative ability, greatly improved overall productivity, and a new level of integration of industrial processes and information technology.

The implementation of the plan will expand the scope for cooperation between China and the rest of the world in a joint effort to propel new progress in the global manufacturing sector.

国家大数据战略

大数据是以容量大、类型多、存取速度快、应用价值高为主要特征的数据集合。2014年3月，大数据首次写入中国中央政府工作报告；2015年10月，中共十八届五中全会正式提出“实施国家大数据战略，推进数据资源开放共享”。这表明中国已将大数据视作战略资源并上升为国家战略，期望运用大数据推动经济发展、完善社会治理、提升政府服务和监管能力。此举可以促使中国政府从“权威治理”向“数据治理”转变，促进政府与民众的沟通互联，提高政府应对各类事件和问题的智能化水平。同时，中国希望通过推行国家大数据战略，加快大数据发展核心技术研发及应用，重构国家综合竞争优势，赢得未来发展先机。

The National Big Data Strategy

Big data can be characterized by the huge volume, the wide variety, the extreme velocity at which data are processed, and the high value that big-data technologies can create.

The issue of big data was discussed for the first time in the Report on the Work of the Government delivered in March 2014. At its fifth plenary session in October 2015, the 18th CPC Central Committee unveiled a national big data strategy that promotes open exchange and sharing of data. The need for such a strategy underscores the increasing importance of big data as a strategic asset on China's development agenda. The strategy calls for exploring the potential of big-data technologies to boost economic growth, and improve governance at all levels, as well as government services and regulation.

This move will enable the Chinese government to switch from an authority-based approach to governance to a data-based approach. It will not only create a higher level of interaction with the public, but also enhance the ability of the government to respond to exigencies and solve problems with the aid of smart data technologies. The implementation of this strategy is also expected to accelerate big data related core technology research, development and application, so as to enhance China's national competitiveness and pave the way for future development.

中国（上海）自由贸易试验区

中国（上海）自由贸易试验区于2013年9月29日在上海浦东外高桥挂牌成立。这是中国在新形势下推进改革开放的一项重大举措，旨在为全面深化改革和扩大开放探索新路径、积累新经验，促进各地区共同发展。试验区的总体目标是：经过两至三年的改革试验，加快转变政府职能，积极推进服务业扩大开放和外商投资管理体制改革，大力发展总部经济和新型贸易业态，加快探索资本项目可兑换和金融服务业全面开放，探索建立货物状态分类监管模式，努力形成促进投资和创新的政策支持体系，着力培育国际化和法治化的营商环境，力争建设成为具有国际水准

China (Shanghai) Pilot Free Trade Zone

The launch of the China (Shanghai) Pilot Free Trade Zone at Waigaoqiao, Pudong, Shanghai, on September 29, 2013, was a major reform move in response to China's new realities. It was aimed at exploring new possibilities for expanding the scope of reform and opening China wider to the outside world, and promoting coordinated development of all regions.

Within a two- to three-year window, the pilot program was, in broad terms, expected to expedite the transformation of government functions, push for the opening of the service sector and foreign investment regulatory reform, encourage the development of a headquarters economy and new types of trade, and speed up RMB capital account convertibility and the opening up of financial services. Its objectives also included developing a mechanism for tariff classification of merchandise, building a support framework that encourages investment and innovation, and fostering a business environment in which international norms and the rule of law are respected. The program sought to create a world-class free trade zone

的投资贸易便利、货币兑换自由、监管高效便捷、法制环境规范的自由贸易试验区，为中国扩大开放和深化改革探索新思路和新途径。试验区的主要任务是按照先行先试、风险可控、分步推进、逐步完善的方式，形成与国际投资、贸易通行规则相衔接的基本制度框架，涉及加快政府职能转变、扩大投资领域开放、推进贸易发展方式转变、深化金融领域的开放创新、完善法制领域的制度保障等五方面。同时，试验区还致力于营造相应的监管和税收制度环境。

with convenience for investment and trade, full convertibility of currencies, an efficient regulatory mechanism, and an effective legal environment. It could provide fresh ideas for further reform and opening up.

The pilot program would be implemented step by step with adequate attention to risk control in an attempt to develop a framework in line with international norms for investment and trade. Areas of focus were envisioned as follows:

- accelerating the transformation of government functions;
- opening more areas to foreign investors;
- promoting the transformation of trade development approach;
- further opening the financial services industry, and encouraging innovation; and
- improving legal and institutional arrangements.

In addition, work on an appropriate regulatory and taxation framework would also be pursued.

京津冀协同发展

京津冀协同发展是中国的重大国家战略，其核心是有序疏解北京非首都功能，调整经济结构和空间结构，探索出一种人口经济密集地区优化开发的模式，促进区域协调发展，走出一条发展的新路子。京津冀协同发展的范围包括北京市、天津市以及河北省的保定等11个地级市，环保、交通和产业升级转移是三个重点领域。中国政府发布的《京津冀协同发展规划纲要》的突出特点是，通过寻求发展来解决环境和社会经济问题，同时也通过环境的约束性为发展打下基础。

Coordinated Development for the Beijing-Tianjin-Hebei Region

Coordinated development for the Beijing-Tianjin-Hebei region, as part of China's development strategy, aims at orderly relocating all non-essential functions from Beijing, the national capital, to neighboring locations. The move entails adjusting the economic structure and rationalizing space utilization, while exploring a new mode of optimized integrated development in a region with a dense population.

The broad region covers Beijing, Tianjin and 11 prefectural cities in the neighboring Hebei Province. Environmental protection, integrated transport services, and industrial upgrading and relocation are the three focus sectors. The Outline of the Plan for Coordinated Development for the Beijing-Tianjin-Hebei Region, released in April 2015, highlights development-oriented solutions to ecological, social, and economic problems, and incorporates considerations of environmental sustainability in development planning.

亚洲基础设施投资银行

2013年10月，中国国家主席习近平提出了筹建亚洲基础设施投资银行（简称亚投行）的倡议。随后，中国与相关国家开展协商谈判。2014年10月24日，包括中国、印度、新加坡等在内21个首批意向创始成员国的财长和授权代表在北京签约，共同决定成立亚投行。2015年12月25日，历经800余天筹备，由中国倡议成立、57国共同筹建的亚洲基础设施投资银行正式成立。它是一个有政府间性质的亚洲区域多边开发机构，重点支持基础设施建设，旨在促进亚洲区域建设互联互通和经济一体化的进程，并且加强中国及其他亚洲国家和地区的合作。它也是一个开放、包容的多边开发银行，欢迎所有有兴趣的域内外国家加入，共同为促进亚洲地区基础设施建设和经济发展做出贡献。

Asian Infrastructure Investment Bank

The idea of establishing the Asian Infrastructure Investment Bank (AIIB) was first unveiled by President Xi Jinping of China in October 2013. Consultations and negotiations between China and other interested countries followed shortly. An agreement on establishing the AIIB was signed in Beijing on October 24, 2014, by finance ministers or envoys from the first 21 AIIB prospective founding members, including China, India, and Singapore. The bank was formally established on December 25, 2015, after more than 800 days of joint preparatory efforts by 57 countries.

The AIIB is a regional inter-governmental development institution focused on supporting Asian infrastructure development, regional connectivity and economic integration, and strengthening cooperation between China and other countries and regions. The Bank's openness and inclusiveness reflect its multilateral nature. The AIIB welcomes the participation of all countries in Asia and beyond in efforts to contribute to Asian infrastructure and economic development.

外交篇

Foreign Affairs

和平共处五项原则

1954年，中国、印度、缅甸共同倡导了互相尊重主权和领土完整、互不侵犯、互不干涉内政、平等互利、和平共处五项原则。这是国际关系史上的重大创举，为推动建立公正合理的新型国际关系作出了历史性贡献。和平共处五项原则生动反映了联合国宪章宗旨和原则，并赋予这些宗旨和原则以可见、可行、可依循的内涵。60多年来，历经国际风云变幻的考验，和平共处五项原则作为一个开放包容的国际法原则，集中体现了主权、正义、民主、法治的价值观。新形势下，中国将继续坚持和弘扬和平共处五项原则，同国际社会一道，推动建设持久和平、共同繁荣的和谐世界。

The Five Principles of Peaceful Coexistence

In 1954, China, India and Burma jointly proposed the Five Principles of Peaceful Coexistence, namely, mutual respect for sovereignty and territorial integrity, mutual non-aggression, non-interference in each other's internal affairs, equality and mutual benefit, and peaceful coexistence. The enunciation of these principles was a major initiative in the history of international relations and a significant contribution to the building of a new type of just and equitable international relations.

The Five Principles of Peaceful Coexistence give concrete expression to the purposes and principles of the UN Charter and facilitate their implementation. Having been tested by the evolution of international relations in the past six decades, they have become general principles of international law, which reflect openness and inclusiveness, and emphasize the importance of respect for sovereignty, justice, democracy and rule of law.

In this new era, China will continue to uphold and promote the Five Principles of Peaceful Coexistence and work with the international community to bring lasting peace, prosperity, and harmony to the world.

和平发展道路

和平发展道路归结起来就是：既通过维护世界和平发展自己，又通过自身发展维护世界和平；在强调依靠自身力量和改革创新实现发展的同时，坚持对外开放，学习借鉴别国长处；顺应经济全球化发展潮流，寻求与各国互利共赢和共同发展；同国际社会一道努力，推动建设持久和平、共同繁荣的和谐世界。中国将坚定不移走和平发展道路，同时也将推动各国共同坚持和平发展。中国将积极承担更多国际责任，同世界各国一道维护人类良知和国际公理，在世界和地区事务中主持公道、伸张正义。中国主张以和平方式解决国际争端，反对各种形式的霸权主义和强权政治，永远不称霸，永远不搞扩张。中国主张坚持共赢精神，在追求本国利益的同时兼顾别国利益，做到惠本国、利天下，推动走出一条合作共赢、良性互动的路子。

Peaceful Development

The concept of peaceful development is underpinned by a focus on seeking peaceful development with the help of a peaceful international environment while also contributing to the maintenance of world peace through our own development initiatives; relying on our own efforts, particularly through reform and innovation, to achieve progress while also opening wider to the rest of the world and learning from the experiences of other countries; adapting to the process of economic globalization and seeking mutual benefits for all; and working with the international community to bring lasting peace, prosperity, and harmony to the world.

China's commitment to peaceful development is unshakable, and we encourage all other countries to do the same. We will take on more international responsibilities, work with other countries to uphold humanity's best interests and international norms, and stand for justice in regional and international affairs. International disputes should be resolved by peaceful means. Never seeking hegemony or pursuing an expansionist foreign policy ourselves, we oppose all forms of hegemony and power politics. It is our consistent position to encourage the search for win-win solutions that take into account the interests of other countries as well as those of our own, and are beneficial to all. It is essential to foster cooperative interaction among members of the world community.

中国改革开放30多年的历史已经证明，和平发展是中国基于自身国情、社会制度、文化传统作出的战略抉择，顺应时代潮流，符合中国根本利益，符合周边国家利益，符合世界各国利益。

As China's experience of reform and opening up over the past 30-plus years shows, the pursuance of peaceful development has been a crucial strategic move that is based on the considerations of China's national conditions, social system and cultural traditions. It represents a timely response to today's imperatives and serves the fundamental interests of China, and those of its neighbors and the rest of the world.

维护国家核心利益

中国走和平发展道路、倡导合作共赢是以坚决维护国家核心利益为底线的。中国的核心利益包括：国家主权，国家安全，领土完整，国家统一，中国宪法确立的国家政治制度和社会大局稳定，经济社会可持续发展的基本保障。习近平总书记指出："我们要坚持走和平发展道路，但决不能放弃我们的正当权益，决不能牺牲国家核心利益。任何外国不要指望我们会拿自己的核心利益做交易，不要指望我们会吞下损害中国主权、安全、发展利益的苦果。"

Safeguarding the Core Interests of China

China's commitment to peaceful development and mutually beneficial cooperation is underpinned by its determination to safeguard its national core interests. These interests include state sovereignty, national security, territorial integrity, national reunification, stability of its political system established by the Constitution and overall social stability, and the need to ensure sustainable economic and social development.

At a meeting of the Political Bureau of the CPC Central Committee in January 2013, General Secretary Xi Jinping reaffirmed China's commitment to peaceful development. This commitment is however premised on the absence of any encroachment upon our national core interests, he added. We will never give up our legitimate rights and interests. No foreign country should harbor the illusion that we would trade our core interests, or allow harm to be done to our sovereignty, security or development.

新型国际关系

2015年9月28日，在世界反法西斯战争胜利和联合国成立70周年之际，中国国家主席习近平首次登上联合国讲台，向世界清晰阐述了以合作共赢为核心的新型国际关系理念。他提出，“我们要继承和弘扬联合国宪章的宗旨和原则，构建以合作共赢为核心的新型国际关系，打造人类命运共同体。”建立平等相待、互商互谅的伙伴关系，营造公道正义、共建共享的安全格局，谋求开放创新、包容互惠的发展前景，促进和而不同、兼收并蓄的文明交流，构筑尊崇自然、绿色发展的生态体系，上述“五位一体”，构成了新型国际关系的主要体系。构建新型国际关系，是中国领导人对攸关人类前途命运的诸如和平与发展等关键问题给出的中国答案。以合作共赢为核心，蕴含着对实现世界和平、发展、公平、正义、民主、自由等全人类共同价值的关怀，亦是对联合国崇高目标的深刻思考。

A New Model of International Relations

On September 28, 2015, Chinese President Xi Jinping spoke for the first time at the United Nations Headquarters. He elaborated to an international audience his concept of building a new model of international relations based on cooperation for the benefit of all.

He said: "We should renew our commitment to the purposes and principles of the Charter of the United Nations, build a new model of international relations based on cooperation for the benefit of all, and create a community of shared future for mankind." He called on the international community to build partnerships based on equality, consultation and mutual understanding, to create a security architecture that is fair, just, and shared by all, to pursue open, innovative, and inclusive development that benefits all, to increase inter-civilizational exchanges that promote harmony in diversity and are mutually enriching, and to encourage ecological conservation and protection, putting Mother Nature and green development first.

Building a new model of international relations is China's answer to tackling the key issues crucial to the future of humankind, such as peace and development. A focus on cooperation in search of win-win solutions embodies China's commitment to world peace, development, fairness, justice, democracy, and freedom – values cherished by humanity and informing the lofty mission of the United Nations.

命运共同体

命运共同体是中国国家主席习近平提出的重要理念之一。截止到2015年5月，他已经60多次公开谈到这一理念。2013年3月，他在莫斯科国际关系学院演讲时，第一次明确提出这一理念。他说："这个世界，各国相互联系、相互依存的程度空前加深，人类生活在同一个地球村里，生活在历史和现实交汇的同一个时空里，越来越成为你中有我、我中有你的命运共同体。"

2015年3月，他在博鳌的演讲中，提出了迈向命运共同体的"四个坚持"：坚持各国相互尊重、平等相待，坚持合作共赢、共同发展，坚持实现共同、综合、合作、可持续的安全，坚持不同文明兼容并蓄、交流互鉴。早在2013年3月，他在访问坦桑尼亚时谈到："这段历史告诉我们，中非从来都是命运共同体，共同的历史遭遇，共同的发展任务，共同的战略利益把我们紧紧联系在一起。"

Community with a Shared Future

Building a community with a shared future is one of the key ideas proposed by Chinese President Xi Jinping. By the end of May 2015, he had spoken about this topic on more than 60 occasions. In an address at the Moscow State Institute of International Relations in March 2013, he brought up this idea for the first time. He said, "It is a world where countries are linked with and dependent on one another at a level never seen before. Mankind, by living in the same global village in the same era and on the same earth where history and reality meet, has increasingly emerged as a community with a shared future in which everyone has in himself a little bit of others."

In his keynote speech at the Boao Forum for Asia Annual Conference in March 2015, President Xi set forth the principles for building a community with a shared future, namely the need for all countries to respect one another and treat each other as equals, cooperate in search of win-win solutions and common development, achieve common, comprehensive, collaborative, and sustainable security, and maintain mutually enriching and beneficial interactions among civilizations in a spirit of inclusiveness. Earlier in March 2013 during his visit to Tanzania, he said that history shows that China and Africa have always found themselves facing similar odds. Similar historical experience, common development tasks and shared strategic interests have bound us together.

共建网络空间命运共同体

2015年12月16日，在中国乌镇召开的第二届世界互联网大会上，习近平发表主旨演讲，重点论述了“网络空间命运共同体”的理念。他说，网络空间是人类共同的活动空间，网络空间前途命运应由世界各国共同掌握。实际上，这一理念在习近平2014年致首届互联网大会的贺词中就已经提到。本届会议期间，他再度提及并进一步提出了共建网络空间命运共同体的5点主张：第一，加快全球网络基础设施建设，促进互联互通。第二，打造网上文化交流共享平台，促进交流互鉴。第三，推动网络经济创新发展，促进共同繁荣。第四，保障网络安全，促进有序发展。第五，构建互联网治理体系，促进公平正义。共建网络空间命运共同体，这是中国领导人在互联网领域提出的中国主张，也需要国际社会共同努力才能实现。

Jointly Building a Community with a Shared Future in Cyberspace

In his keynote speech at the Second World Internet Conference (WIC) in Wuzhen, China, on December 16, 2015, Xi Jinping outlined his vision for a community with a shared future in cyberspace, a vision he first brought up in his message to the First WIC in 2014. He said that since cyberspace as a sphere of human activity belongs to humanity, its future should be decided by all countries of the world. In a five-point proposal for building a cyberspace community with a shared future he highlighted the need to (a) accelerate the development of a global Internet infrastructure and promote interconnectivity; (b) create online platforms to facilitate cultural exchanges; (c) promote the development of the Internet economy and encourage innovation; (d) ensure Internet security and orderly development; and (e) build a cyberspace governance system to ensure fairness and justice.

The goal of building such a cyberspace community, as proposed by China's leadership, can be achieved only through joint efforts by the international community.

总体国家安全观

2014年4月，习近平在主持召开中央国家安全委员会第一次会议时强调，坚持总体国家安全观，以人民安全为宗旨，以政治安全为根本，以经济安全为基础，以军事、文化、社会安全为保障，以促进国际安全为依托，走出一条中国特色国家安全道路。

贯彻落实总体国家安全观，必须既重视外部安全，又重视内部安全，对内求发展、求变革、求稳定、建设平安中国，对外求和平、求合作、求共赢、建设和谐世界；既重视国土安全，又重视国民安全，坚持以民为本、以人为本，坚持国家安全一切为了人民、一切依靠人民，真正夯实国家安全的群众基础；既重视传统安全，又重视非传统安全，构建集政治安全、国土安全、军事安全、经济安全、文化安全、社会安全、科技安全、信息安全、生态安全、资源安全、核安全等

A Holistic View of National Security

In April 2014, while presiding over the first meeting of the National Security Commission of the CPC Central Committee, Xi Jinping emphasized the need to take a holistic view of national security. Through such an approach, a full spectrum of security issues are assessed, ranging from human security, which is the ultimate concern, political security, which is of overarching importance, and economic security, which underpins all other considerations, to military, cultural and social perspectives, which reinforce efforts in other areas, and the promotion of international security, which provides support for measures taken in a national context. Along this line of thinking we are setting out to build a national security system with Chinese characteristics.

Such a holistic approach calls for a focus on both internal and external security. Internally, it is essential to promote development, continue reform, maintain stability, and create a safe environment. Externally, we should promote international peace, seek cooperation and mutual benefit, and strive to bring harmony to the world. Homeland security and the security of our citizens are both of paramount importance. All initiatives taken in this respect will be people-centered, and implemented for the people, on the basis of the people's needs, and

于一体的国家安全体系；既重视发展问题，又重视安全问题，发展是安全的基础，安全是发展的条件，富国才能强兵，强兵才能卫国；既重视自身安全，又重视共同安全，打造命运共同体，推动各方朝着互利互惠、共同安全的目标相向而行。

with the support of the people. Security issues, both traditional and non-traditional, will be taken into account. The national security system we envisage will integrate not only political security and homeland security, but also security-related military, economic, cultural, and social concerns, science and technology, and information, ecological, resource, and nuclear security. Development issues will be considered in tandem with security issues. Development provides a basis for security, whereas security constitutes a necessary condition for development. Only a prosperous country can build a strong military, and only a strong military can defend our country. Our national security must also be viewed in the context of international security. For the sake of our international community with a shared future, we should all work towards our goal of satisfying the world's security needs in a way that is beneficial to all.

新型亚洲安全观

2014年5月，习近平主席在上海举行的亚信峰会上，提出了共同安全、综合安全、合作安全、可持续安全的亚洲安全观。他建议，创新安全理念，搭建地区安全合作新架构，努力走出一条共建、共享、共赢的亚洲安全之路。共同安全，就是要尊重和保障每一个国家安全。综合安全，就是要统筹维护传统领域和非传统领域安全。合作安全，就是要通过对话合作，促进各国和本地区安全。可持续安全，就是要发展和安全并重以实现持久安全。

New Asian Security Concept

Addressing the Fourth Summit of the Conference on Interaction and Confidence Building Measures in Asia held in Shanghai in May 2014, Chinese President Xi Jinping introduced an Asian security concept that emphasizes joint and comprehensive measures and cooperation in ensuring sustainable security. He proposed creating a regional security cooperation framework under the new concept, one that aims at carving a path through joint efforts to a secure future in Asia enjoyed by all. A focus on common security means that the security needs of every country should be respected and duly met. Comprehensive measures should be taken to ensure security in both traditional and non-traditional fields. Cooperation and dialogue are indispensable to strengthening the security of both individual countries and the region as a whole. Sustainable security is possible only when security measures are implemented in conjunction with sustained development efforts.

维护和发展开放型世界经济

中国倡导维护和发展开放型世界经济，主张各国应进一步扩大相互开放，旗帜鲜明地反对各种形式的贸易保护主义，齐心协力做大世界经济这块大蛋糕。为此，各国应维护自由、开放、非歧视的多边贸易体制，不搞排他性贸易标准、规则、体系，避免造成全球市场分割和贸易体系分化。要探讨完善全球投资规则，引导全球发展资本合理流动，更加有效地配置发展资源。

Maintaining and Developing an Open World Economy

China is committed to maintaining and developing an open world economy. It encourages all countries to open their doors wider, stand firm against protectionism in all its forms and work in concert to promote the growth of the world economy. To this end, they should work for a free, open and nondiscriminatory multilateral trading system, and resist any standards, rules or policies that condone or encourage exclusionary trade practices. Efforts are called for to avoid undue fragmentation of the global market and trading system. All avenues should be explored to improve global investment rules, and ensure rational flows and more effective allocation of global development resources.

完善全球经济治理

中国提出的完善全球经济治理的根本目标是推动经济全球化朝着均衡、普惠、共赢的方向发展。均衡，就是要兼顾发达国家和发展中国家需求，平衡发达国家和发展中国家关切。普惠，就是要把各种实实在在的利益和好处带给所有国家，惠及各国人民。共赢，就是要把本国利益同他国利益结合起来，把本国发展同各国共同发展联系起来。全球经济治理应该由世界各国共同参与，特别是增加新兴市场国家和发展中国家的代表性和发言权。

Improving Global Economic Governance

The goal of improving global economic governance is, in our view, to transform economic globalization into a balanced, win-win process that bring benefits to all. The process has to be balanced so as to accommodate the needs of both developed and developing countries, and address their concerns. It should ensure that real results and benefits will accrue to all countries and their people. It should be a win-win game in which the interests and development needs of individual countries are interlocked and coordinated. Global economic governance requires the participation of all countries, and in particular enhanced representation of and a bigger say for emerging-market and developing countries.

正确的义利观

中国主张，在国际关系中，要妥善处理义和利的关系。政治上，要遵守国际法和国际关系基本原则，秉持公道正义，坚持平等相待。经济上，要立足全局、放眼长远，坚持互利共赢、共同发展，既要让自己过得好，也要让别人过得好。

习近平主席指出：义，反映的是我们的一个理念。这个世界上一部分人过得很好，一部分人过得很不好，不是个好现象。真正的快乐幸福是大家共同快乐、共同幸福。中国希望全世界共同发展，特别是希望广大发展中国家加快发展。利，就是要恪守互利共赢原则，不搞我赢你输，要实现双赢。中国有义务对贫穷的国家给予力所能及的帮助，有时甚至要重义轻利、舍利取义，绝不能惟利是图、斤斤计较。正确义利观承继了中国外交的优良传统，体现了中国特色社会主义国家的理念。

The Greater Good and Self-Interest

China views the relationship between the greater good and self-interest as an essential aspect of international relations. At the political level all countries should abide by international law and the basic norms governing international relations, and uphold the principles of fairness, justice, and equality among nations. At the economic level they should seek a course of action that brings mutual benefits and leads to win-win solutions with a focus on an overall picture and long-term considerations.

The pursuit of the greater good remains, as President Xi Jinping once said, embedded in our values. It is not acceptable that the divide between the haves and have-nots perpetuates itself. True happiness should be shared and enjoyed by all. China hopes that all countries in the world, especially developing countries, would benefit from development efforts. The pursuit of self-interest should, on the other hand, be aligned with the need to search for mutual benefit, rather than being turned into a zero-sum game. China has the obligation to provide assistance to poor countries within the limits of its own resources. It is sometimes necessary to work for the greater good at the expense of self-interest and fulfill this obligation despite an unfavorable calculus in financial terms. A healthy approach to the relationship between the greater good and self-interest is grounded in China's tradition of diplomacy, and embodies the values we cherish.

“共同但有区别的责任”原则

“共同但有区别的责任”发端于上世纪70年代初。1972年斯德哥尔摩人类环境会议宣示，保护环境是全人类的“共同责任”；会议同时指出，发展中国家的环境问题“在很大程度上是发展不足造成的”，这已是“共同但有区别的责任”的雏形。1992年，《联合国气候变化框架公约》第四条正式明确了这一原则。根据这个原则，发达国家要率先减排，并向发展中国家提供资金和技术支持；发展中国家仍以经济和社会发展及消除贫困为首要和压倒一切的优先事项，在得到发达国家技术和资金支持的情况下，采取措施减缓或适应气候变化。

这一原则也一直是中国参与国际气候谈判的基础。

The Principle of "Common But Differentiated Responsibilities"

The principle of "common but differentiated responsibilities" began to win general acceptance in the early 1970s. The United Nations Conference on the Human Environment, held in Stockholm in 1972, declared that the protection and improvement of the human environment was the duty of the whole world. It also drew attention to the fact that environmental deficiencies in developing countries are themselves generated by the conditions of underdevelopment. This concept constitutes an essential element of the principle of "common but differentiated responsibilities."

The principle was written into Article 4 of the United Nations Framework Convention on Climate Change adopted in 1992. Under this principle, developed countries should take the lead in emissions reduction and provide support in terms of finance and technology to developing countries, while developing countries should apply this financial and technological support to actions designed to mitigate or adapt to climate change. Notwithstanding, economic and social development and poverty eradication still remain the first and overriding priorities for the developing world.

China has never forsaken this principle in any of the international climate negotiations in which it has participated.

中国的核安全观

2014年3月24日，在荷兰海牙举行的第三届核安全峰会上，中国国家主席习近平发表重要讲话，首次全面阐述了中国的核安全观。其主要内容可以概括为四句话：一是发展和安全并重，以确保安全为前提发展核能事业。二是权利和义务并重，以尊重各国权益为基础推进国际核安全进程。三是自主和协作并重，以互利共赢为途径寻求普遍核安全。四是治标和治本并重，以消除根源为目标全面推进核安全努力。此外，中国还承诺，为实现持久核安全，愿意继续作出自己的努力和贡献。由此，中国成为第一个正式提出核安全观的国家。

China's Views on Nuclear Security

At the Third Nuclear Security Summit that opened in The Hague on March 24, 2014, Chinese President Xi Jinping delivered a speech to expand on China's views on nuclear security:

First, the international community should place equal emphasis on development and security, and develop nuclear energy on the premise of security.

Second, it should place equal emphasis on rights and obligations, and move forward the international nuclear security process on the basis of respecting the rights and interests of all countries.

Third, it should place equal emphasis on independent and collaborative efforts, and seek universal nuclear security through mutually-beneficial cooperation.

Fourth, it should place equal emphasis on treating symptoms and addressing causes, and advance the cause of nuclear security in all respects with the goal of removing the associated risks at the root.

Xi promised that China will continue its efforts to achieve lasting nuclear security.

His speech made China the first country to publicly unveil its views on nuclear security.

交流互鉴的文明观

中国倡导交流互鉴的文明观，其核心内涵是：文明是多彩的，人类文明因多样才有交流互鉴的价值；文明是平等的，人类文明因平等才有交流互鉴的前提；文明是包容的，人类文明因包容才有交流互鉴的动力。当今世界，人类生活在不同文化、种族、肤色、宗教和不同社会制度所组成的世界里，各国人民形成了你中有我、我中有你的命运共同体。应该推动不同文明相互尊重、和谐共处，让文明交流互鉴成为增进各国人民友谊的桥梁、推动人类社会进步的动力、维护世界和平的纽带。应该从不同文明中寻求智慧、汲取营养，为人们提供精神支撑和心灵慰藉，携手解决人类共同面临的各种挑战。

Exchanges and Mutual Learning Between Civilizations

China promotes exchanges and mutual learning between civilizations. Such exchanges and mutual learning are necessitated by the diverse nature of civilizations, premised on the principle of equality, and propelled by a healthy dose of inclusiveness.

While the world we inhabit is characterized by diversity in terms of culture, ethnicity, skin colors, religions and social systems, people across the world increasingly find themselves in a community with a shared future, with their interests interlocked. It is therefore crucial to promote mutual respect and harmonious coexistence between civilizations. Exchanges and mutual learning can be a bridge of friendship between peoples, a driver of progress for humanity and a bond of world peace. There is great promise in tapping the wisdom and power of world civilizations to find moral support and cultural inspiration for our joints efforts to address challenges facing humanity.

"一带一路"

"一带一路"是"丝绸之路经济带"和"21世纪海上丝绸之路"的简称。2013年9月和10月，中国国家主席习近平出访中亚和东南亚时，分别提出了与相关国家共同建设"新丝绸之路经济带"和"21世纪海上丝绸之路"的倡议。该倡议以实现"政策沟通、设施联通、贸易畅通、资金融通、民心相通"为主要内容，以共商、共建、共享为原则，实实在在地造福沿线国家和人民。

"一带一路"主要涵盖东亚、东南亚、南亚、西亚、中亚和中东欧等国家和地区。"一带一路"建设符合有关各方共同利益，顺应地区和全球合作潮流，得到了沿线国家的积极响应。截止到2016年7月底，已有70多个国家和国际、地区组织表达了支持和参与"一带一路"建设的积极意愿，30多个国家和国际组织与中国签署了共建"一带一路"政府间合作协议。

The Belt and Road Initiative

The Belt and Road Initiative, also known as the Land and Maritime Silk Road Initiative or the "One Belt, One Road" Initiative, refers to China's proposal to build a Silk Road Economic Belt and a 21st Century Maritime Silk Road. During his visits to Central and Southeast Asia in September and October 2013, respectively, Chinese President Xi Jinping unveiled the plans to implement this initiative in cooperation with related countries. The initiative is based on five conceptual pillars – policy coordination, connectivity of facilities, unimpeded trade, financial integration, and strengthened people-to-people ties – and on the principle of mutual discussion, building jointly, and sharing the benefits equally, so as to bring genuine happiness to the people along the belt and road.

The coverage area of the initiative is primarily East Asia, Southeast Asia, South Asia, West Asia, Central Asia, and East-Central Europe. Building the Silk Road Economic Belt and the 21st Century Maritime Silk Road is for the common interest of all regions involved, and conforms to the trend of regional and global cooperation, having already received active responses from the countries along the belt and road. By July 2016 over 70 countries and international and regional organizations had expressed their support for and willingness to participate in the initiative, and more than 30 countries and international organizations had reached agreements to cooperate with China in building the Silk Road Economic Belt and 21st Century Maritime Silk Road.

丝绸之路精神

历史上的商业通道——丝绸之路，作为人文社会的交往平台，多民族、多种族、多宗教、多文化在此交汇融合。千百年来，丝绸之路承载的和平合作、开放包容、互学互鉴、互利共赢精神薪火相传。中国与丝绸之路沿线国家在维护民族尊严、捍卫国家主权的斗争中相互支持，在探索发展道路、实现民族振兴的道路上相互帮助，在深化人文交流、繁荣民族文化的事业中相互借鉴。习近平主席提议，新时期弘扬丝绸之路精神，就是要促进文明互鉴、尊重道路选择、坚持合作共赢、倡导对话和平。

The Spirit of the Silk Road

The historical trade route known as the Silk Road was also a platform for people-to-people and cultural exchanges, where people from various ethnic, racial, religious and cultural backgrounds met and assimilation occurred. Embodying peace, cooperation, openness, inclusiveness, eagerness to learn from each other, and mutual benefit, the spirit of the Silk Road has been passed down through generations for thousands of years. China and other countries along the Silk Road have all along supported and helped each other in their efforts to defend national dignity and sovereignty, explore approaches to development, and bring about national renewal. By learning from each other, they have benefited from expanded people-to-people and cultural exchanges and national cultural revitalization drives.

President Xi Jinping proposed a new initiative to promote the Silk Road spirit in the new era to boost interaction and exchanges between civilizations. The initiative calls for respect for the chosen approaches to development of individual countries, and promotion of peace through mutually beneficial cooperation and dialogue.

丝路基金

2014年11月8日，中国国家主席习近平宣布，中国将出资400亿美元成立丝路基金。丝路基金将为“一带一路”沿线国基础设施建设、资源开发、产业合作等有关项目提供投融资支持。它同其他全球和区域多边开发银行的关系是相互补充而不是相互替代的，将在现行国际经济金融秩序下运行。丝路基金绝非简单的经济援助，而是通过互联互通为大家的发展创造新的重大发展机遇。丝路基金是开放的，欢迎亚洲域内外的投资者积极参与。它的成立，将会助推“一带一路”建设和亚洲地区互联互通。

Silk Road Fund

On November 8, 2014, President Xi Jinping announced that China would invest US$40 billion to set up the Silk Road Fund. The Fund will support the development of infrastructure and resources, and industrial cooperation, among other projects, in the countries along the land and sea Silk Roads. It will serve as a complement to, rather than a substitute for, other global and regional multilateral development banks, and will operate under the existing international economic and financial order.

Instead of simply dispensing economic aid, the fund will create major development opportunities for all through increased connectivity. It is open and welcomes the active participation of investors from Asia and beyond. Its establishment will spur the implementation of the Belt and Road Initiative and promote regional connectivity.

构建中美新型大国关系

2013年6月，中国国家主席习近平与美国总统奥巴马在安纳伯格庄园会晤，提出共同努力构建中美新型大国关系。关于中美新型大国关系的内涵，习主席在会晤中用三句话作了概括：一是不冲突、不对抗。二是相互尊重。三是合作共赢。不冲突对抗，是构建中美新型大国关系的必要前提。相互尊重，是构建中美新型大国关系的基本原则。合作共赢，是中美构建新型大国关系的必由之路。

Developing a New Model of Major-Country Relations Between China and the United States

Meeting with President Barack Obama of the United States at the Annenberg Retreat in California in June 2013, President Xi Jinping of China proposed building a new model of major-country relations. This new model, in his words, boils down to three principles: (a) no conflict or confrontation, which is a prerequisite; (b) mutual respect, which provides the basis for healthy major-country relations; and (c) mutually beneficial cooperation, which provides the means to turn this vision into a reality.

瀛台会晤

2014年11月11日晚，中国国家主席习近平同美国总统奥巴马在北京中南海瀛台就中美关系及共同关心的重大国际和地区问题，进行了坦诚、轻松的非正式会晤。两国元首以瀛台漫步的轻松形式展开了长时间的会晤。习近平借古喻今，向奥巴马讲述了古老瀛台的历史由来。他说，当代中国人的思维、中国政府的治国方略，浸透着中国传统文化的基因。中美国情各异，历史文化、发展道路、发展阶段不同，应该相互理解，相互尊重，聚同化异，和而不同。奥巴马总统对此回应道，会谈加深了他对中国的国情以及中国政府和领导人执政理念的了解，更加理解中国人民为何珍惜国家统一和稳定，美国无意遏制或围堵中国，愿意同中方坦诚沟通对话，增进相互了解，欢迎中国在国际事务中发挥建设性作用，愿同中方携手应对各种全球性挑战，共同

The Xi-Obama Meeting at Yingtai

Chinese President Xi Jinping had a candid, relaxed, and informal meeting with U.S. President Barack Obama on the evening of November 11, 2014 at Yingtai, an island with ancient palace buildings within the Zhongnanhai compound. They discussed issues concerning Sino-US relations and other major global and regional issues of mutual concern.

The two heads of state had a long, relaxed conversation while strolling at Yingtai. Xi told Obama about the history and anecdotes of Yingtai. The DNA of traditional Chinese culture is, in Xi's words, embedded in contemporary Chinese thinking and in the governance strategies of the Chinese government. Diverging national contexts of the two countries with regard to history, culture, development paths, and stages of development, he noted, underscore the importance of mutual understanding, mutual respect, and tolerance for differences in the search for common ground and lasting peace. In response Obama acknowledged that the talk had enabled him to gain a better insight into China's realities and the governance philosophy of the Chinese government and its leaders, and a better understanding of the aspirations of the Chinese people for national unity and stability. Debunking the notion that the United States seeks to contain China, he reiterated his willingness to have a candid dialogue with China so as to foster mutual understanding,

促进亚太和世界和平与安全。瀛台会晤是继中美两国元首在美国加州安纳伯格庄园举行“不打领带”的非正式会晤后，中美首脑外交的又一创新安排，有利于双方在战略层面理解彼此意图，增进战略互信，展现了中美两国致力于构建中美新型大国关系的决心。

and welcomed China as a constructive player in international affairs in the shared endeavor to address global challenges and promote peace and security in the Asia-Pacific region and the world.

The talk at Yingtai, a continuation of the open-necked informal summit at the Annenberg Retreat in California, represented another innovative diplomatic engagement at the most senior level between China and the United States. The event helped both sides foster mutual trust and better gauge each other's intentions at a strategic level, and further demonstrated the imperative for both governments to work towards a new model of major-country relationship.

提升中欧全面战略伙伴关系

中欧是当今世界两大力量、两大市场、两大文明。在世界多极化、经济全球化、文化多样化、国际关系民主化的时代背景下，中欧合作更具全球性、战略性、示范性，对推动国际力量平衡、促进世界和平与发展意义重大。2014年4月，习近平主席在布鲁日欧洲学院发表演讲时提议：要建设和平稳定之桥，把中欧两大力量连接起来。建设增长繁荣之桥，把中欧两大市场连接起来。建设改革进步之桥，把中欧两大改革进程连接起来。建设文明共荣之桥，把中欧两大文明连接起来。

Upgrading the China-EU Comprehensive Strategic Partnership

China and the European Union (EU) are two influential players on the international stage and two major markets, and represent two major civilizations. Against the backdrop of growing multi-polarity, economic globalization, increasing cultural diversity and greater democracy in international relations, Sino-EU cooperation assumes greater importance as a strategic model for the rest of the world in shaping the balance of power in international relations and promoting world peace and development.

Addressing the College of Europe in Bruges in April 2014, Chinese President Xi Jinping proposed building a bridge of peace and stability linking the two influential players, a bridge of growth and prosperity linking the two big markets, a bridge of reform and progress linking the reform processes in China and the EU, and a bridge of cultural prosperity linking the two major civilizations.

“亲、诚、惠、容”的周边外交理念

“亲、诚、惠、容”是中国与周边国家发展关系提出的重要理念。周边国家在中国外交总体格局中占据首要位置和极为重要的战略意义。稳定安宁的地区环境，是中国和周边国家的共同期许。无论是从理智上还是从感情上，中国都认为与邻为善、以邻为伴是唯一正确的选择。因此，中国主张亲、诚、惠、容的周边外交理念。所谓亲，就是坚持睦邻友好，守望相助；讲平等，重感情；常见面，多走动；多做得人心、暖人心的事，增强亲和力、感召力、影响力。所谓诚，就是诚心诚意对待周边国家，争取更多朋友和伙伴。所谓惠，就是本着互惠互利的原则同周边国家开展合作，编织更加紧密的共同利益网络，让周边国家得益于中国发展，使中国也从周边国家共同发展中获得裨益和助力。所谓容，就是倡导包容的思想，强调亚太之大容得下大家共同发展，以更加开放的胸襟和更加积极的态度促进地区合作。

Building Relations with Neighboring Countries Based on Friendship, Good Faith, Mutual Benefit, and Inclusiveness

Topping China's foreign policy agenda is the need for building relations with neighboring countries based on friendship, good faith, mutual benefit, and inclusiveness. It is an issue of strategic importance. China and its neighbors share an aspiration to foster a stable and peaceful regional environment. Both logic and cultural affinity point to the wisdom of a good-neighbor policy. It is therefore China's wish to build ties with neighboring countries on such a basis.

Friendship involves good-neighborly interactions, mutual support and assistance, and frequent reciprocal visits, and is informed by equality, cultural affinity, and empathy. It contributes to stronger ties, and enhances the appeal of our region as a whole and its impact on world affairs. Good faith is required in working with our neighbors. We need more friends and partners. Mutual benefit is the foundation on which China cooperates with its neighbors. It helps strengthen networks for those who share common interests, and enables China and its neighbors to benefit from each other as they pursue their development strategies. Inclusiveness is indispensable to regional cooperation. Underpinned by the belief that the Asia-Pacific region is large enough to accommodate us all, it encourages open-mindedness as we work more proactively towards our shared goals.

对非“真、实、亲、诚”

2013年3月，习近平主席在达累斯萨拉姆发表演讲，总结中非友好关系发展历史经验，全面阐述了新时期中非共谋和平、同促发展的政策主张。第一，对待非洲朋友，讲一个“真”字，始终把发展同非洲国家的团结合作作为中国对外政策的重要基础。第二，开展对非合作，讲一个“实”字，只要是中方作出的承诺，就一定会不折不扣落到实处。第三，加强中非友好，讲一个“亲”字。中非人民有着天然的亲近感，要更加重视中非人文交流，积极推动青年交流，使中非友好事业后继有人。第四，解决合作中的问题，讲一个“诚”字，中方坦诚面对中非关系面临的新情况新问题，本着相互尊重、合作共赢的精神加以妥善解决。

Building Relations with Africa Based on Sincerity, Real Results, Friendship, and Good Faith

In his speech in Dar es Salaam, Tanzania, in March 2013, Chinese President Xi Jinping summarized the history of Sino-African friendship and the experience of developing such a friendship, and elaborated on his proposals for concerted efforts to promote peace and development in the new era.

First, China has a sincere desire to build strong ties with its African friends. Solidarity and cooperation with African countries have always been an important part of China's foreign policy. Second, cooperation with Africa has been and will continue to be results-oriented. China will honor every commitment it makes to Africa. Third, the traditional and intimate friendship between the Chinese and African peoples will continue to be strengthened. Efforts will be made to expand people-to-people exchanges, especially youth exchange programs, so that our friendship can be passed on to younger generations. Fourth, we will always act in good faith in addressing problems that might occur in our relations with Africa. New developments and issues relating to our bilateral relations will be discussed frankly and dealt with on the basis of mutual respect and through mutually beneficial cooperation.

中非全面战略合作伙伴关系

2015年12月5日，中国国家主席习近平在中非合作论坛约翰内斯堡峰会上，全面阐述了中国对非关系政策理念，提出把中非关系由“新型战略伙伴关系”提升为“全面战略合作伙伴关系”。它由五大支柱支撑，即政治上的平等互信，经济上的合作共赢，文明上的交流互鉴，安全上的守望相助，国际事务中的团结协作。为推进这一关系建设，习近平还同时提出了未来三年中方将同非方重点实施的“十大合作计划”，涉及工业化、农业现代化、基础设施、金融、减贫惠民等领域，这为中非全面战略合作伙伴关系建设夯实了基础。中非全面战略合作伙伴关系的确立，彰显了中国将秉持“真实亲诚”的对非政策理念和义利观，同非洲大陆携手迈向合作共赢、共同发展的新时代。

China-Africa Comprehensive Strategic and Cooperative Partnership

Speaking at a summit of the Forum on China-Africa Cooperation (FOCAC), President Xi Jinping of China outlined China's policy toward Africa and proposed that the new type of China-Africa strategic partnership be upgraded to a comprehensive strategic and cooperative partnership. The partnership is underpinned by five major pillars, namely, political equality and mutual trust; mutually beneficial economic cooperation; cultural exchanges; security cooperation and mutual assistance; and solidarity and coordination in international affairs.

In this regard, Xi also proposed joint implementation of a 10-point plan in the next three years. The plan covers industrialization, agricultural modernization, infrastructure, financial support, and poverty reduction, among others. It provides a basis for building the comprehensive partnership. The vision for an upgraded partnership reflects China's desire to forge relations with Africa based on sincerity, real results, friendship and good faith, and to serve the greater good. It is a vision for a new era of China-Africa mutually beneficial cooperation and common development.

图书在版编目（CIP）数据

中国关键词．第一辑：汉英对照 / 中国外文出版发行事业局，中国翻译研究院著；韩清月等译．— 北京：新世界出版社，2016.8（2023.2 重印）

ISBN 978-7-5104-5938-2

Ⅰ．①中… Ⅱ．①中… ②中… ③韩… Ⅲ．①中国特色社会主义 – 社会主义建设模式 – 研究 – 汉、英 Ⅳ．① D616

中国版本图书馆 CIP 数据核字 (2016) 第 204311 号

中国关键词（第一辑）

项目策划：张海鸥
作　　者：中国外文出版发行事业局　中国翻译研究院
翻　　译：韩清月　徐明强　蔡力坚
责任编辑：赵如意
特约编辑：李　旭
改　　稿：David Ferguson（英）
审　　定：徐明强　蔡力坚
校　　对：张丽娟
责任印制：王宝根
出　　版：新世界出版社
网　　址：http://www.nwp.com.cn
社　　址：北京西城区百万庄大街 24 号（100037）
发 行 部：(010)6899 5968（电话）(010)6899 0635（电话）
总 编 室：(010)6899 5424（电话）(010)6832 6679（传真）
版 权 部：+8610 6899 6306（电话）nwpcd@sina.com（电邮）
印　　刷：天津中印联印务有限公司
经　　销：新华书店
开　　本：880mm×1230mm　1/32　尺寸：95mm×200mm
字　　数：100 千字　　　　　　印张：7.5
版　　次：2016 年 8 月第 1 版　2023 年 2 月第 10 次印刷
书　　号：ISBN 978-7-5104-5938-2
定　　价：68.00 元